"Families grieve a loss, but how do we mark the loss of the families we create—friends, teachers, students, colleagues? Rabbi Greyber's story touches each of us who mourn, and his wisdom helps us cope with our own bewilderment and grief."

—Rabbi David Wolpe, author of *Why Faith Matters*

Faith Unravels

Faith Unravels

A Rabbi's Struggle with Grief and God

Rabbi Daniel Greyber

RESOURCE *Publications* · Eugene, Oregon

FAITH UNRAVELS
A Rabbi's Struggle with Grief and God

Resource Publications
An Imprint of Wipf and Stock Publishers
199 W. 8th Ave., Suite 3
Eugene, OR 97401
www.wipfandstock.com

ISBN 13: 978-1-62032-199-7
Manufactured in the U.S.A.

Grateful acknowledgment is made to the following:

The Rabbinical Assembly for allowing me to re-print sections of "Sheloshim is Over" and "A Letter from Camp Ramah in Ojai" which were previously published in *Conservative Judaism*.

The United Synagogue of Conservative Judaism for allowing me to re-print "Praying for the Sick, Praying With the Sick," previously published in *CJ Voices* Fall 2008.

Sandy Rosen and Amy Musher, parents of Jay Rosen, for their permission to publish Jay's poem, *Blind Faith*.

Rabbi Bradley Shavit Artson for his permission to reprint a section of his letter to the Ziegler School community following Joel Shickman's death.

For Jay Rosen and Joel Shickman.

"How the mighty have fallen!" (2 Samuel 1:27)

Contents

Foreword

by Mayim Bialik

WHEN MY GRANDMOTHER DIED, my family was surprised when I told them that I arranged for her to be buried in her mother's nightgown, a plain cotton garment embroidered with her initials. No one had known that such a garment existed. But I knew, because during the time I got to know her and care for her in the years before she died, she had told me all about it. I alone knew where to find the nightgown, and I alone knew how much it meant to her.

I was responsible for my grandmother's life in many ways, tending to her business and personal affairs because my father and his brother did not take on this responsibility. I was also responsible for the arrangements after her death, arranging a traditional burial, complete with a *shomer*, someone to accompany her body, all the way from Los Angeles to her resting place in Florida. I was my grandmother's friend, business manager, and confidante.

When I spoke at her funeral, I sought to declare my grief and prove my intimacy with her in life and in death. So I listed things that were a part of her life that only *I* knew: her favorite foods, things she liked to talk about, things she worried about. Why did I feel the need to show how close I was to her? Because a grandchild is not obligated to follow Jewish mourning practices (a spouse, child, parent, and sibling are the only relatives designated as mourners by Jewish law). Since traditional Jewish ways of showing allegiance were closed to me, I sought to show my closeness in any way I could. What I wanted to do was to mourn for my grandmother the way Judaism had taught me. Instead, I felt like a second-class griever. I grieved *for* my father and his brother's loss when I wanted to grieve *with* them.

During my grandmother's final years, I met Rabbi Daniel Greyber. He was a fledgling Rabbi at UCLA Hillel, and I was a student at the time.

We baked challah for Shabbat and attended some campus events together. He was mostly "the cute, tall young Rabbi" and I was mostly "the girl from 'Beaches' and 'Blossom' who hangs out at Hillel." We didn't talk then about how I visited my grandmother weekly and helped her pay bills. We didn't discuss what it was like to file her nails, handle her health insurance, or help her navigate a life predicament she never really wanted. I didn't ever imagine when I spoke to Rabbi Greyber that he knew about what it was like to want to be a part of someone's life and death but not know how to do it practically. As it turns out, he knew a lot about that.

Rabbi Greyber has done something magnificent with the book you are holding in your hands. He has shared of himself, revealed in the most intimate way where loss can take you, and where it can't. He has allowed us a peek inside a world of religious observance, beauty and joy and, in doing so, laid bare the profundity of Judaism. This book is not preachy or full of instructions. It's a personal testament of love for the Jewish people, God and those friends he loved and lost.

When my grandmother left this world, I was singing to her, a Hebrew poem I learned from my Hillel years before. She stirred, something shifted in the air, and the next moment, I knew she was gone. I was alone in the room with her tiny body in my arms. I stopped singing.

There is a moment we know a soul departs the body. But there is also a moment in our grief when we know we are no longer alone, that there is hope beyond sadness and love beyond despair. In hearing someone else's story that reminds us of our own, we find the strength to start over again and love even more deeply because we have lost. Reading this book was such a moment for me. I hope you find in its words the comfort that I have.

Acknowledgments

WE MOURN ALONE. YET we are not without recourse. There is comfort we can give, words and experiences we can share alongside one another, like rocks thrown across the ravine that let others know we are here. I am grateful for those with whom I was privileged to share the joy of Jay and Joel's lives, the pain of their illnesses and deaths, and the struggle to recover meaning and faith again.

I am particularly grateful to Heather, for the friendship our families have shared since she and Joel and their boys moved to Los Angeles in 2005; for allowing me to help, and be helped by, her throughout Joel's sickness and death, and who so graciously gave permission for these words to come to light so that they might be a comfort to others who mourn.

I am grateful to Jay's parents, Sandy Rosen and Amy Musher, and Jay's brother, Jeffrey, for their blessing when we wanted to name our third son after Jay, for their permission and support in helping this story come to life, and for our friendship, which has extended over many years.

I am grateful to Rabbi Bradley Shavit Artson, Reb Mimi Feigelson, Dr. Pinchas Giller and so many other teachers and friends whose counsel I sought, and whose Torah and wisdom sustained me during my grief. I began to write this book while I was still the Executive Director of Camp Ramah in California. I am grateful to the Board and staff who supported me during Joel's illness and the grief that followed. Mistakes in this book are my own, but this book was immeasurably improved by many colleagues and teachers from Los Angeles who read early drafts and offered loving guidance and support including Miriyam Glazer, Naomi Levy, Deborah Silver and David Wolpe. While in Los Angeles, I was blessed with wonderful *talmidim-chaverim*, people who were both students and friends, who read and re-read this book, and whose questions and conversations helped this story come to light: Tom Fields-Meyer, Steven Klein, Amy Mendelsohn, Erika Resnick, and Lindsay Stricke-Bressman. While in Los Angeles we met two friends who happen to be stars, both of whom agreed to help spread word about this book because they wanted to help bring comfort to people in pain. I am grateful to Mayim Bialik who generously agreed to write the foreword for this book—for her teaching of our eldest son, for her continuing friendship, and for the wonderful Jewish voice she brings into the world. Thank you also to Brad Delson and his family for their friendship, for their love of Jewish life, and for the prayers we sang together.

After leaving Ramah in August of 2010, I was blessed to spend the year as a Jerusalem Fellow at the Mandel Leadership Institute. I am grateful to Morton L. Mandel, whose vision created the Mandel Foundation and whose family sustains it as a place that invests in Jewish education for the future. During that year in Jerusalem, Abigail Dauber-Sterne directed the Jerusalem Fellows program with depth and wisdom, encouraged my work on this book, and offered helpful suggestions. I am grateful to the other 2010–11 Jerusalem Fellows: Daniel Moses, who read several drafts and shared his counsel with me at many Jerusalem cafes, Tanya Podolnay, Ruthie Rotenberg, Ofer Sabath Beit Halachmi, and Debra Shaffer Seeman. I am grateful for the shared table around which we argued and for your continuing interest in my ups and downs while writing and re-writing. While in Jerusalem, I met new teachers and friends many of whom read this book and offered more helpful advice including Allan Finkelstein, Frani Hecker, Avraham Infeld and Daniel Marom. I first met Daniel Gordis when I expressed interest in the Ziegler School in the fall of 1996. Since then, I have been blessed to be his student and friend, and reuniting with him and gaining his advice on this book while in Jerusalem was yet another blessing of a wonderful year. Finally, a few weeks after arriving to Israel, I discovered that our upstairs neighbor, Brian Blum, was an editor. I am grateful to Brian who coaxed the story out of me and helped the words to say what I hoped they would.

The year in Israel would never have been possible were it not for the generosity of our new community at Beth El Synagogue in Durham, North Carolina. James Tulsky and David Reed didn't hang up the phone when I asked if the synagogue would consider my spending a year at Mandel *before* beginning as Beth El's full-time rabbi. It was their belief in me, along with that of the rest of the community that made possible our family's year in Israel when this work truly came together. Since our family's arrival in Durham, Sandy Kessler not only served as Beth El's President, helping me learn how to be a congregational rabbi, but also took a keen interest in this book and offered helpful advice in its later stages. Thank you to Lisa Feld for her gentle expertise, which helped me sharpen the final draft and navigate the world of permissions. To Jared Resnick and his family, new friends who have taught me much about loss, love and giving of ourselves again. To Jacki and Mike Resnick who have known too much loss, for allowing me to be one of their many rabbis, and for giving me the gift of solace in the North Carolina mountains so I could complete the final draft of this work.

My father always said, "Write a book." Well, here it is Dad. Thank you for instilling in me the hunger to bring light to the world and the belief that I could. It was my mom who put the book in my bag so long ago that urged me to ask the questions about what life means, and who nurtured within me a belief that I might have an answer worth sharing. To my sister who has suffered her brother becoming a rabbi and reminded me of times when I wasn't: thank you for the marathons to fight cancer, and for your holy work as a doctor working to beat the damn disease. To my brother, my companion: you too have walked this road, stood too many times at a friend's grave. To the summer of your life, and remembering those who died in springtime. To my sons, Alon, Benjamin and Ranon: it is you who showed me that hope persists, and what for. May God bless you with long life. To my wife Jennifer, my life's love, and my best friend when tears would not cease, there are no words to thank you enough. Finally, this work would be incomplete without offering thanks to the Creator for the courage to continue to write, and sing, and love, for I can love completely, without complete understanding.

Passover, 1982

A FEW DAYS AGO in Hebrew school they showed us a black and white movie. There was a bulldozer and lots of dead bodies. We learned the word "Holocaust" and the number "six million." Tonight my sister reads from the Hagaddah across our long dining table: "God brought us out of Egypt not by an angel, not by a seraph, not by a messenger, but the Holy Blessing One, God Himself in His glory..." For just a moment, I wonder: "Why didn't God save all those people in the movie?" But I was the child who did not know how to ask. So I ate matzah ball soup, sang "Dayenu," forgot the question, and even that it ever occurred to me to ask.

chapter 1

Jay

"Two are better than one; because they have a good reward for their labor. For if they fall, the one will lift up his fellow: but woe to him that is alone when he falls; for he has no other to help him up."

—ECCLESIASTES 4:10

1

December 1996

OUR FAMILY GATHERS IN San Jose, California. We spend the day at my sister's home waiting for her to give birth to her first son, Ari. He finally arrives in the evening. We head to the hospital to celebrate and return to her home for a festive dinner when my brother pulls me aside. "Jay died this morning. The funeral is tomorrow. I'm so sorry, Daniel."

I make flight reservations with TWA and a few hours later I am on a red-eye from San Francisco through St. Louis to Washington-Dulles. At the funeral, Jay's coffin is lowered into the grave, *kaddish* (the Jewish memorial prayer) is said, family and then friends are invited to put dirt on the coffin. I approach and the rabbi hands me—an athlete in the prime of my youth—a small spade with some dirt and explains that placing dirt in the grave is a way of "symbolically helping with the burial." I take the spade and meekly turn it over. A little dirt falls in.

A small car is waiting. I sit in the back right-hand seat; there are four of us, healthy young guys. We are quiet and the car idles. Soft earth rests beneath the tires. We wait for a line of cars to creep forward, away from the graves. I turn and look through the rear-view window.

A few people mill around the tent where the family sat, while three men dressed in dark green uniforms casually shovel earth into Jay's fresh, open grave. An impulse rises in me—one I remember to this day with regret, un-acted upon. I want to open the car door, walk over, and take a shovel, move the professionals aside, and do it all myself. I want Jay to be buried by people who knew and loved him, not people paid to do it.

Sitting in the car, I realize I don't want a damn symbol. I want the thing itself, not just a spade. I want to dig deep into the mound of earth, lift a full shovel, and strain to swing it over to the grave. Now, I yearn to get out of the car, move the gravediggers aside and dirty my shoes, to breathe hard and sweat through my shirt. I want to dump earth onto his coffin and fill the space where he will rest forever, like tucking in a child at night. That is what one does for a brother. That is what we do for those we love. But it is only a thought in my mind. The car creeps forward, and the four of us drive away in silence across the winding streets of Northern Virginia.

We return to Jay's mom's home. His parents got divorced in high school. Like most kids, Jay was bitter, and happy for them too, that they should be happy. I remember walking the suburban neighborhood streets with him, talking it through, thinking that perhaps Jay's battle with leukemia had kept them together and driven them apart; that the years of illness and sadness, of treatments and watching your child struggle and suffer, were finally too much. People gather in the living room. I remember the house, but the room is unfamiliar. Jay and I would play pinball or wrestle in his basement. We would play basketball in his driveway. We never spent any time in the living room.

2

The Shiva House

I know a little about how Jews mourn. I am 25 years old and three of my four grandparents are already dead. Grandpa Sam was the official photographer for the Oakland Raiders and a semi-pro golfer. I remember driving in the front seat of his big brown Cadillac and chasing after balls while he played a round of golf. When Grandpa Sam died, I was eight. My parents left me in Potomac and flew to California for a week. I stayed with a family that had a house with a long driveway and I learned to ride a bike.

Grandpa Arthur fought in World War One and could calculate his grocery bill to within a few cents even though he never went to college. He wore an orange sweater jacket and I thought he looked dignified when he walked with a cane. When my grandpa Arthur died, I was eleven. Our family used to drive four hours north to their home in Queens, New York to visit. I remember returning from the funeral to my grandmother's musty apartment and crying inconsolably. My mom was surprised at how strongly I was reacting to the loss, until I explained that in the commercial for Country Time Lemonade there was always a grandpa who sat on the porch and drank Country Time with his grandson, but now I didn't have any grandpas anymore.

My grandma Beatrice was a classical pianist and taught hundreds of people to play the piano. I wasn't her best student, though she tried. By the time I saw her play piano, arthritis made her hands clumsy and stiff, yearning but unable to produce music now locked within. Shortly after my bar mitzvah, Grandma Beatrice got sick during a visit to our home in Maryland. When the decision was made to take her off the ventilator, they thought she would die in minutes. But my older sister—now a doctor, then only 17 years old—sat next to her hospital bed, held her hand, and coached her to live: "Breathe, Grandma, breathe. You can do it!" She lived a few days more instead of a few hours; but then she died. I was 13 years old. After that, we didn't travel to New York anymore.

We cling to an illusion of safety. We try to protect ourselves by believing death happens according to a schedule. When we are young and a grandparent dies, we tell ourselves, "Death happens to people who are old. I am young so I am okay." Jay's death took away from me the luxury of illusion. Death has its own schedule.

I learned about *shiva* from my grandparents' deaths. *Shiva* is a seven-day period of mourning beginning after a funeral. Mourners aren't supposed to leave the house, bathe, shave, have sex, or drink alcoholic beverages. The community makes prayer services, brings meals and visits the mourners' home. Too often, people do not know what to do or say, so they avoid coming altogether, or they say things that are more hurtful than helpful. Jewish tradition teaches we should enter the home, sit quietly, and let the mourner begin the conversation. But many people are scared of silence, so they talk instead.

I also learned that the only people who are required to "sit" *shiva* are family. The Jewish legal tradition defines a mourner as one of seven relatives: mother, father, sister, brother, son, daughter, or spouse. It is a bit strange, but being obligated to do something in Judaism matters more than doing it because you want to. So if you're not required to mourn by Jewish tradition—for example, a friend is not required to mourn—it's like your mourning matters less. A friend's job is to provide comfort, not receive it.

So, sitting in Jay's living room, I feel it is my and my friends' responsibility to comfort Jay's younger brother, mom, and dad—his family. I feel this way not because of anything Jay's family said to me, but because it is what I've been told is Jewish tradition. I am sad and bewildered. But in light of that tradition, those feelings strike me as selfish. I don't sit and cry; I help with the food instead. I speak about Jay when other people share stories. Later that afternoon, the meal concludes, the service ends. I hug Jay's family and spend some time with my friends outside the house.

As "just" a friend and not a family member, Jewish tradition seems not to allow for my sadness and grief, so I say goodbye, drive back to the airport and try to move on. As I look out the airplane window on the flight across the country, I need someone who understands what it is to lose a friend at a young age. I need someone who can tell me I am not alone. But I am.

This is not the book I planned to write; it is the one I needed to write. It is for the 25 year-old me who drove away from Jay's grave not knowing how to bury him, who helped Jay's family but did not know how to help myself; did not know that the Jewish tradition could in fact support me in my grief. It is for those who have made the journey to, and back from, the funeral of a friend, but struggled with the return to life.

3

I met Jay in 10th grade; he was in remission after having spent middle school fighting leukemia. Jay was a brilliant guy. He passed seventh, eighth and ninth grade while undergoing chemotherapy. In our senior year of high school, Jay was part of a three-member team on *It's Academic*, a quiz bowl televised on Sunday mornings by the local NBC affiliate. Jay and the team from Churchill High School in Potomac, Maryland won the championship our senior year. I sometimes think that part of the reason for our strong friendship was that I got to know him as a healthy person, rather than as "the boy with leukemia."

We were in a few classes together, and would skip school some afternoons and play basketball until I had to go to swim practice. After senior prom, we took our dates to his dad's boat in Annapolis where his dad brought us breakfast and took us out on the Chesapeake Bay at dawn. I remember that morning; I was swimming in the fresh bay waters, feeling the slow roll of the waves wash over me, coaxing Jay to come in the water. He rarely swam—maybe he was self-conscious of his slight body and felt himself more put-together on dry land. But for whatever reason that morning, Jay, who was usually too stubborn to be convinced, decided to swim with me. I remember looking at him floating gently on his back underneath a warm sunny sky, and thinking to myself, "He deserves this."

Jay attended Northwestern University. I went to Berkeley but transferred to Northwestern my junior year. We decided to room together. The relationship was rocky sometimes - we both had changed and grown since high school - but it was good to feel "known." We were enjoying a great year; I was on the swim team, he was involved in student government. But that February, Jay came out of remission and returned home to battle cancer again. He had a bone marrow transplant that summer, and returned to campus in the fall for our senior year. Jay finished his undergraduate degree and, having finally graduated, was offered a dream job working in sports media in London.

Things were looking up; Jay had fought and won again, and he reveled in the blessing of just being healthy and getting ready to live a normal life. To get an apartment and have a job and live on his own! It was exciting for all of us, but for Jay, after years of dependence and weakness and debilitation, the prospect of an "ordinary" future was a dream fulfilled.

That spring, Jay left for London. I returned to Northwestern in the fall for a year of graduate work and to finish my swimming career. We corresponded only occasionally. In my last few weeks at Northwestern, I got a call. Jay had to return home to Potomac from London. It wasn't cancer, but Jay was feeling weak and having trouble walking. It was something they did not understand. When I came home a few weeks later, he was walking with a cane.

4

Summer 1994

I returned home from Northwestern to Potomac, Maryland, a suburb of Washington, D.C., to coach the team I swam on as a child. When my parents arrived in Potomac, I was just a baby and it still felt like "horse country" from Colonial America. There were beautiful old homes with large, green yards. Ours had a white picket fence. By the time I graduated high school, small farms in the surrounding area had been transformed into housing developments and there was a Starbucks in the Potomac Village Shopping Center.

Potomac Pool had been renovated, but it still retained its character, set amidst a forest of old trees and still populated by children who spent six or eight hours a day just hanging around the pool like I did as a child. As coach, I revived old cheers that were being forgotten and swam workouts with the older kids to stay in shape. I was lucky enough to have a summer to give back, to fulfill a dream of coaching the team at a pool I loved. At the final banquet, with friends and family looking on, I got a chance to say thank you—not just for the summer, but for a childhood of memories.

On evenings off from swim coaching, I visited Jay at his house. We drank Cokes, watched Orioles games and sat at the piano together while he pounded out chords to songs of Billy Joel and Elton John. He was a short—5 foot, 3 inches—his growth stunted from struggling with leukemia and its treatments since seventh grade. But he looked smaller, thinner than before. I would visit him every few weeks. Sometimes we would meet at a pizza place. He would ask about the pool, about coaching, and the team. Jay exchanged a cane for a walker. He stopped meeting me out of the house. By summer's end, the walker could not help him anymore; he was bed-bound.

I knew Jay was in a fragile state, but I also wanted to get on with my own life. "It's not the first time he's been sick," I told myself. I wasn't hard to convince. So, in September, I boarded a plane and headed off to Israel.

Why Israel? When I went away to college my freshman year, my mom hid in my bags a book by Rabbi Harold Kushner called, *When All You've Ever Wanted Isn't Enough: The Search for a Life That Matters*. It was a university assignment of a different sort. My mom had read it over the summer, probably because I was the last child to leave home and she was becoming an "empty nester," about to experience the exhilarating, terrifying freedom of being more than "just a mom" after so many years of hard work raising me and my siblings. The quiet. The serenity. The fear. Rabbi Kushner's book begins:

> A man sat opposite me in my study one evening…[and] told me what was on his mind.
> "Two weeks ago, for the first time in my life, I went to the funeral of a man my own age…He died suddenly over the weekend…That was two weeks ago. They have already replaced him at the office… Two weeks ago he was working fifty feet away from me, and now it's as if he never existed. It's like a rock falling into a pool of water. For a few seconds, it makes ripples in the water, and then the water is the same as it was before, but the rock isn't there anymore. Rabbi, I've hardly slept at all since then. I can't stop thinking that it could happen to me, that one day it will happen to me, and a few days later I will be forgotten, as if I had never lived. Shouldn't a man's life be more than that?"
> … This book is written to help people cope with another, more subtle kind of tragedy, the disease of boredom, meaninglessness, a sense of the futility and purposelessness of our lives.

Reading Rabbi Kushner's book as a freshman did not provoke in me a radical change in lifestyle. I stayed in school, went to parties, and continued my swimming career. But I began to wonder about the meaning of my life, what made me special, how I would leave a mark, or if my life would be like that rock that sinks to the bottom of the pond and is swallowed up, as if it never was.

I started to wonder about religion. I read more. When I was growing up I thought that observant Jews had it easy and that I was the one who *really* struggled. I thought that they just accepted God's existence and were acting like robots, unquestioningly following orders. That may be how some observant Jews are, but the Pulitzer Prize-winning Jewish-American author Herman Wouk challenged me to consider religion not as a means to avoid struggle, but rather as a pathway towards deepening our wrestling with life's most important questions. In his spiritual autobiography, *This is My God*, Wouk writes, "Let me suggest that the words 'I may be wrong' are words that our present day needs, outside Judaism as within it. We are overloaded with shallow certainties. But where are the deep doubters? To echo the agnostic questions of the past two centuries is not to doubt, but to recite classroom lessons." Reading his book, I asked myself whether all my life I'd used my doubts to keep me safe outside of Judaism. Wouk dared me to consider, "I may be wrong," to risk asking deeper questions from the inside.

I could say I went to Israel to explore Judaism, to look for meaning. But really, at the end of the summer, as I sat at Jay's hospital bed and saw how fragile life is, I think I was just scared. Scared of taking a job. Scared of getting an apartment and becoming a commuter. Scared of doing what everyone else did. I was scared of getting married and getting a house and having kids and buying a mini-van and getting promoted and waking up 15 years later in Rabbi Kushner's office wondering, "Shouldn't my life be more than this?" So I left Jay in his hospital bed and went off to find myself.

6

To the outside world, I imagine my life seemed perfect. I had been captain of the Northwestern University swim team where I held school records. I'd received my Master's degree in Communications. Now I was headed to Israel for a year of post-college study at the WUJS Institute (the World Union for Jewish Students) in the northern Negev desert. I was writing the next chapter of my life. A perfect story. What could be wrong? But as the plane climbed over the Atlantic in September, I thought about Jay, whom I was leaving behind. I felt sad, guilty, and self-absorbed. Going to Israel should have felt like a dream; but as the plane started to descend over the Mediterranean coast, all I could think about was Jay in a hospital bed, too sick to walk. The plane landed. I got settled in at WUJS, but I didn't like myself. I had abandoned my friend when he needed me most.

After a few weeks at our home base in Arad, itself a desert town, our group headed south from the northern Negev for a trip to the desert near Eilat at the southern tip of Israel. We spent several days hiking amidst the red, craggy mountains that surround Israel's resort town on the Red Sea. During the days we ascended the mountains and looked out over Egypt, Israel, Jordan and Saudi Arabia, each hugging its own precious strip of rich blue, coral-filled waters on the Red Sea coast. We ate pomelos—a fruit with an exceptionally thick skin and a taste sweeter than a grapefruit but tarter than an orange—and drank plenty of water at the urging of our Israeli guides who were raised with an almost paranoid obsession with avoiding dehydration. At night we slept in the desert under the stars. Since our trip coincided with Hanukkah, a few of us brought candles. We lit them huddled against small rocky hills that protected the flames against the strong night desert wind.

I remember watching the candles flicker back and forth, the wicks struggling to stay lit, and how much light they gave off amidst the darkness. I thought about being in Israel and being a Jew and about how many people in my family had struggled to stay Jewish for thousands of years before me. Against the rocks with some friends, I thought about how, amidst a world of billions of people, it felt like a miracle that the Jewish people had survived. My Jewishness had been passed along like a precious heirloom that made it two thousand years across the world and through history to me, an American boy growing up in suburban Maryland at the end of the twentieth century. We watched the candles for a while, then walked back to the bonfire and ate steak and chicken *al ha'esh* - cooked on large grills stowed under the bus for just this purpose.

On the last night of the trip, thinking about the long bus ride back to Arad the next morning, I sat down around the fire with a large plate of steak kebab and waited for the wine to come around to me. I listened to people chatting and to a few friends who were playing guitar. We started to sing—Don Mclean, Simon and Garfunkel, James Taylor, Billy Joel—songs that had sustained me through high school and college.

A bottle finally arrived and I drank deeply from the wine. My mind started to wander. With each song, I grew into a deeper silence, surrounded by friends but wandering away in my heart and mind, within myself and far away, to my friend back home in a hospital bed. I stood up, took an open bottle of wine in each hand from the stash that had been brought along, and walked away from the fire, over a small rocky hill, and into a vast desert darkness beyond.

Looking back, I could see rays from the fire lighting the top of the hill I had just descended. I could hear the sounds of the guitars and the singing, slightly masked by a slow but cool desert wind. I walked on, climbed another 30-foot, craggy mound, and descended into a narrow depression lower than the fire and lower than the area between the two hills I had climbed. Here, I was sheltered from the wind, the voices and the music of the guitar. The beams of the fire were left behind. No moon had yet risen.

I leaned my body against the sharp, steep slope, uncorked one of the bottles and took a long, large drink from the bottle. I stopped, breathed out, looked around and was not afraid; I felt a deep anger welling up within me and took the bottle again, gulping, a swallow, another, another, and did not taste the sourness of the wine going down. I drank more and started to breathe heavily, exhaling with great force through my mouth. I bent over and gripped the slender neck of the second bottle in my right hand, swung it behind me and heaved it high over the surrounding ridge and cried out a long guttural scream. I flailed my arms, swung wildly in a circle, and wailed, "Why?!!!!!"

My heart pounded and my chest heaved. I lowered myself to my knees on the dry ground and started to sob, long and deep. My eyes and nose ran. I buried my head in my hands, and cried without inhibition. My breathing slowed. I wiped my eyes and nose with my shirt sleeve, held my knees, and looked up at a sky vast and dark, bright stars without measure. I felt surrounded by darkness, but not smothered. I could feel and breathe the darkness but I was not scared. Like a blanket surrounding me, I felt I was being held, comforted, even soothed, by a great vastness, an awesomeness I could not deny. It was there, I believe, I felt God's presence for the first time. Or rather, that He was thrust upon me.

chapter 2

Becoming a Rabbi

1

I AM A RABBI who got suspended from Hebrew school in 3rd grade. When my parents took me to synagogue on Saturday mornings, we sang what to me were Hebrew songs that I learned through sheer repetition of the melodies week after week. When the cantor finished singing, I sat down and looked around, not knowing if there was something I was supposed to do while he and the rabbi stood quietly for a moment. At that time, it never occurred to me that prayer could involve *me*, that it *should* involve me. Prayer was an activity done by professionals, by others. It was words on a page of a strange book in an ancient language I did not understand. There were melodies I came to know—nice tunes—but not music that moved me and expressed how I truly felt inside, like when I was an awkward teenager and James Taylor reassured me "You've Got a Friend." The synagogue melodies were tunes one could hum and that passed the time, but they left me untouched.

Growing up, I was taught—not explicitly, but through what happened or did not happen—that prayer occurred in discrete places, inside a sanctuary, say; at discrete times, on a Friday night or a Saturday morning; and was done by discrete people, the rabbi and cantor. I dressed up in a suit and wore a tie that made it hard to breathe. I was told to sit still and listen, or, when I was a teenager, I was told I could go outside. So I left, and wandered the halls of the synagogue in exile, learning to flirt with girls and going back inside to ask my parents when we could go home.

Like many American Jewish teenagers, I completed my bar mitzvah—I even stuck around a few extra years until 10th grade Confirmation—and then, when I went away to college, I dropped out of Jewish life. I did not do so out of spite or anger, I just dropped out. It would be a mistake to say that when I went to college in 1989, I left Judaism. I left a lot of things—the home I grew up in, my childhood friends, my parents. I left my synagogue and rabbi too, but only because I was growing up and moving on. I did not take a relationship to God with me simply because I did not have one, and it never occurred to me that I could. Services at Hillel, the Jewish students' campus organization, were foreign; they failed to offer the feeling of home I hoped they would. So I immersed myself in life at college. I enrolled in freshman classes and trained on the UC Berkeley swim team and tried to figure out who I was. The thought of God was far from my mind.

Rebbe Nachman of Bratzlav, a Jewish mystic, once taught, "There are two kinds of hiding. When God hides Himself once, it is very hard to find Him. Nevertheless if we work hard, we can find Him because we know He is hidden. But when God hides Himself *within* hidden-ness—meaning that we don't even know that God is hidden from us—then it is nearly impossible to find Him." For the first part of my life, God was not just hidden from me. The fact that God was hidden from me was itself hidden from me.

2

Crying for Jay in the desert was my first encounter with God. It did not last. Sometimes we are blessed with a personal experience of God that feels so real, we can't deny it. But such experiences are fleeting. The Jewish people wander through the Sea of Reeds (Red Sea) and watch God close the walls upon Pharaoh and his army. The next thing, we're complaining of thirst - apparently not convinced that the God who parted the seas could take care of us in the desert. Miracles are hard to come by and they don't last. Most of the time, God is hard to find, much harder to hold on to, so we have to work at it, to train ourselves to sense a hint of God's presence in the world through study, prayer, ritual practice and ethical deeds.

We returned to Arad from our camping trip. On Saturday morning, I stood at the door to the sanctuary at WUJS. It wasn't much of a sanctuary. The floor was dusty and cold. Long fluorescent lights buzzed. Rows of plastic chairs faced a plain wooden ark with one Torah. In the far corner, Rabbi Aubrey Issacs, the WUJS rabbi, stood next to the ark and swayed intensely with a *tallit* (a traditional prayer shawl) over his head. I hesitated at the door. Aubrey fascinated and confused me. His eyes were closed and his lips moved; he appeared to be speaking passionately (but quietly) to the air. What was he thinking about? Did he see an image in his mind? Did he hear a voice answering? Did he see something (Someone!) I did not? Didn't he have questions about whether or not God exists? Was he really saying every word that fast? Did he believe every word he was reading? Did he understand every word? Wouk's challenge echoed in my mind: was I willing to ask these questions from within? I took a prayer book, stepped inside, and tried to follow along.

On Sunday, I began to study. I spent evenings reviewing Hebrew flash cards and only occasionally visited the local bars—there were exactly two in the city, Max's and Muza's. In January, our group traveled to the north of Israel and stopped at Gan Hashlosha, a park set around natural pools that are fed by the Sachne hot springs. I was swimming butterfly, showing off for the girls, when I noticed Jennifer, a good swimmer who told me she used to dive in high school. We flirted, studied, and read books together. Ten months later, Jennifer and I were engaged. One of the things I most appreciated about Jennifer was how—while she arrived to Israel not even knowing how to read Hebrew letters, something I had learned and remembered from Hebrew school—we were both on a journey during those six months in Arad. She embraced my desire to throw myself into learning everything I could about Judaism: law, commentary, prayer, philosophy. Jennifer and I dated. I read as much as I could. I wrote to Jay less often.

Everything in my experience told me that effort and discipline are necessary for things that are worthwhile and endure. One does not simply show up to a swim meet and win. Great performances on one day are the result of weeks and months of labor. To be an artist of anything, one has to invest in learning and practice. It made sense to me that a meaningful Jewish life should be no different. So I studied the *siddur*, the Jewish prayer book, looking back and forth between the English and Hebrew to understand the blessings and psalms in their original. I woke up mornings and tried to pray like Aubrey. I tried keeping Shabbat for the first time and, in the early spring, I celebrated Purim for the first time as an adult.

Growing up, I thought Purim was the Jewish Halloween, our costume holiday. Purim tells the story of how, 2,000 years ago in ancient Persia, a Jewish woman named Esther hides her identity, marries the king, and winds up saving the Jewish people from annihilation at the hands of the wicked Haman. In part to hide our own identities, we dress up to celebrate Purim today. Sometimes our family went to the Sunday Purim carnival at synagogue. I never liked the whole costume part, though. I wasn't going to be Esther. Dressing up as King Achashverosh just meant putting on a crown. I didn't like being Haman because I didn't want someone drawing a mustache on my face. And how did you dress up as Mordecai, Esther's uncle, who sends her to marry the king in the first place? But the games at the carnival were cool and I could usually talk the parents working the booths into giving me more tickets for prizes.

At WUJS, Purim was totally different. First of all, there was a *mitzvah* (literally, a "commandment" in Hebrew) to get drunk—we never did *that* growing up! We also studied the Book of Esther in class during the weeks leading up to the holiday; the story was certainly not a children's fable. King Achashverosh had a party that lasted six months! He told his servants to bring Queen Vashti before him wearing her royal crown (Esther 1:11)—the rabbis said that meant she was to appear wearing her crown, and nothing else! There were parts that seemed downright racy—"Esther approached and touched the tip of the scepter" (Esther 5:2)—this wasn't stuff we learned in Hebrew school.

Aubrey told us the word "king" appears 200 times in the book, but God's name isn't written even once, and that the holiday is a day on which God's presence is hidden (even the name "Esther" is similar to the Hebrew word *hester*, meaning "hidden"). Growing up, most holidays were, "they tried to destroy us. God saved us. Let's eat!" This was different. Getting drunk on Purim was a ritualized reaction to how *hafuch*—upside down—the world feels when God's presence seems hidden. Rather than just a kids' holiday, one tradition taught it was actually the holiest day of the year! Yom Kippur—which we usually think of as the most important day of the Jewish calendar—was called *Yom Ki-Purim* because it is a day like, but not quite equal to, Purim. The days were similar because both are meant to bring you to a place of vulnerability and truth—Yom Kippur through fasting and praying all day, Purim through drinking and laughter.

Some friends and I spent a few hours finding costumes in town. Not Queen Esther and Mordecai, but fun, grown up costumes. The girls looked good. The guys tried to look cool. As the Book of Esther was chanted, whenever Haman's name was read, we didn't just shake noisemakers, we shouted and booed. Some bottles of scotch were passed around the synagogue—this was great! For the first time, I could understand some of what was read so I followed the story as it unfolded. When Haman was hung, we started singing, "Na na na na, hey hey hey, good bye!" The reading ended and the party continued. We drank and sang. Some people danced.

Later in the evening, I found myself sitting by myself, overcome by a profound feeling of gratitude. I was drunk. I felt at home, like I was part of something much larger than myself, that my life mattered more than a stone swallowed up in a pool. I was in Israel celebrating Purim with young Jews from all over the world. I thought about how we had a holiday that embraced doubt, a story without miracles or God, but that was more like the world I lived in, where God's presence was hard to find. I had a lot of doubts, but now, drunk on the floor on Purim, I was doubting from the inside of the tradition.

In Arad, where the sleepy town ends and the Negev desert begins, is a place called "the point." A few days before graduation, I went for a run through town and arrived to "the point" as the final rays of sun warmed my back just before setting below the horizon. My breathing slowed. A slight wind blew in my ears. All else was silent. The desert was painted red and gold. Miles in the distance, thousands of feet below, I saw shimmering light dance on the Dead Sea. Beyond were the mountains of Jordan. Thousands of years before, Moses died and was buried by God, there. "Good day," I said out loud, "good day."

After WUJS ended, I wanted to continue learning, so in the spring and summer of 1995 I studied at a *yeshiva*—a traditional Jewish academy. I bought *tefillin* (phylacteries worn during weekday prayers—see Deuteronomy 6:8, which says "they [the words of the Torah] shall be a sign upon your arm and frontlets between your eyes") and wore them regularly for the first time. I learned to pray each morning and afternoon and took pride when I could eventually lead the prayers. I learned Aramaic—the ancient language in which the Talmud (the preeminent collection of Jewish law and folklore) is written—and followed the rhythms of the *beit midrash*, the traditional Jewish study community. At some point along the way, I found God again, but this time it was different.

It was not crying for Jay beneath a vast desert sky. There was no white light, no deep voice that revealed itself to me. Rather, it was a slow process, like tea steeping in boiling water, gently releasing its flavor. For a long time, I had felt deep inside me that life is meaningful, that the death of an ant is perhaps a loss but not a tragedy, that the death of a person is not merely a loss of a different scale, but of a different quality. The laws of physics and the world provided no rational explanation for this qualitative distinction I felt inside myself, for the aching sensation that what I do with my life matters, not just to me and my family and friends, but in some ultimate way.

From that feeling I came to believe that there is a God who cares about my life, the life of the Jewish people and the world. That belief was not one of total certainty; it was a commitment. From my immersion in Jewish study and prayer and practice, I learned to pay attention to little, everyday moments, like how we eat or talk to a stranger, or how we wake up in the morning, and through those moments, to believe that God is there if we open ourselves up to Him. It was a different kind of encounter, one that emerged out of life lived rather than a temporary moment. It felt like it would last; an enduring faith.

5

In the fall of 1995, I moved to study at a new *yeshiva* in Jerusalem. Jay and I exchanged a few emails—he seemed to be holding steady. My parents told me my childhood rabbi was coming to visit Jerusalem. I contacted him. As we sat in a café drinking *café hafuch*—Israeli for "cappuccino"—I told him I was thinking of becoming a rabbi. He was, rightfully, surprised. But I told him my story: about my questions that began when I read Rabbi Kushner's books, about how I remembered some of his sermons and decided to come here and learn more. I excitedly shared with him my experiences at WUJS and the *yeshivot* and learning to pray and study, and now, how I wanted to return to the United States and be a rabbi. He listened patiently, asked some questions, and shared some advice I did not expect.

"Don't go right away."

"What?" I asked, confused. I thought he would be excited, encouraging, proud! "Why not?"

"Take your time," he explained gently. "I can see how much you've learned, and I'm proud to have played a small role. You are at the beginning of a deep and important journey, Daniel. My sense is that, as you return to the States and begin your life together with Jennifer, you should take time to learn what it is to observe Jewish law—praying, keeping kosher, keeping Shabbat—in the midst of 'regular life.' When you decide to become a rabbi, you don't want to wake up three years into rabbinical school or five years into the rabbinate and discover that you do not like keeping Shabbat. You first want to live the lifestyle and then pick the profession, not the opposite."

It was wise advice. Jennifer and I returned to the States engaged. I started a job in January of 1996 at Leo Burnett, an advertising company in Chicago. During the first week of my first full-time job, I approached my supervisor and nervously explained that I observed the Jewish Sabbath and, for a few months until the sun set later, I would need to leave work early on Friday afternoons, and, "could I please make up the time by coming early or staying late the other days of the week?" She said, "Of course. I respect your integrity and commitment to your traditions. I'm sure we can work around this until the spring."

I traveled to Austin, Texas and Omaha, Nebraska and spent days driving city streets and highways with salesmen from companies that sold billboard advertising to our clients. One morning, I found myself in a hotel in Waco, Texas. Being in Waco felt random. Here I am, a Jew, in Waco! My family was from Russia and Hungary. The story of the Jewish people began in places like Hebron and Jerusalem. What was I doing in Waco? But before the day's meetings began, I walked out near the river that runs through town, took out the compass from my bag, found which way was east and, in Waco, Texas, I turned towards Jerusalem, as the Talmud tells us to do when praying.

As I wrapped the black straps of the *tefillin* around my arm, I thought about something one of my teachers once told me. He said that when he put on *tefillin*, it was like the story of Odysseus who wanted to hear the sirens' song. He ordered his sailors to plug their ears, tie him to the mast and, no matter what he said, not to untie him as they sailed by the island. "The straps of the *tefillin*," my teacher explained, "allow me to listen to the world, to participate in it, without it pulling me away and making me forget who I am." I felt the stare of a few people who walked by and I thought about how I was probably the first person to pray with a *tallit* and *tefillin* on the particular patch of earth that I stood on. But as I prayed, I also felt at home, connected to the Jewish people and tradition, doing what I was supposed to do in some cosmic sense, not just a businessman caught up in the rat race.

On trips like this, I kept kosher as best I could by ordering vegetarian meals at business lunches. I read Jewish books on the plane. Back in Chicago, I studied on the commuter train and prayed in the mornings at a synagogue downtown. Going to prayers *before* work allowed me *to* work. It reminded me that my job, even in its most demanding periods, did not constitute the ultimate meaning of my life. Rather, it was something I enjoyed (or didn't), that allowed me to earn a living, and would eventually allow me to provide for my family; but that I expressed the meaning of my life through my dedication to the Jewish traditions and the Jewish people.

In September of 1996, Jennifer and I flew back to her hometown of Atlanta and got married. We invited Jay. He was too sick to come. It was hard for him even to talk on the phone. Jennifer and I honeymooned in Northern California, then returned back to work and life in Chicago. We enjoyed life in the city, went to some Bulls basketball games. Life was fun, and I was getting used to balancing my work in advertising and Jewish living. It was when we were visiting my family in California that December that my brother told me Jay died.

6

I returned from the funeral to Chicago and went back to morning *minyan* (a quorum of ten Jews that, according to Jewish Law, is required to pray as a group) before work. Most of the people were older or middle-aged men. I wanted to join in saying the mourner's *kaddish*, but it felt wrong, disrespectful. The people who said it had lost one of the seven relatives. If I recited the *kaddish*, people would notice. They would ask me, "who died?" and if I told them, "a childhood friend," I thought they'd wonder, "why is *he* saying *kaddish*?" I felt like I'd be stealing something from them; as if their *kaddish* would be less special if I joined in. So I just listened. When *minyan* was over, people asked me over breakfast, "how was your vacation?"

"It was fine," I replied, and left for work.

Advertising looked different now. I was good at it. Soon I could get promoted and could earn more money. I could go to business school and get an MBA and get an even bigger job. But was this how I wanted to spend so much of my time? I started to think again about being a rabbi. In Israel, I had more than just that one moment in the desert when I cried about Jay. I found an answer to the question from Rabbi Kushner's book long ago. I found a way to forge a life that was meaningful, not just to myself and my friends, but in some more permanent way.

Jay's death taught me that life is impermanent—none of us are going to live forever. In America, everything was modern and new. But in Israel, "new" was only 100 years old! "Old" meant thousands of years. Jewish tradition was old; it was rich with wisdom and authenticity. Rabbis were people who were entrusted with sharing that wisdom with others, helping to pass it on to the next generation. I loved the prayers, loved studying Torah, loved working with other people and thinking about the meaning of our lives. I gave some presentations at work and felt like I was a good public speaker. People said I was a good teacher when I coached the swim team a few summers before—not the same as teaching Torah, but helping people learn seemed like something I could do. I was living the lifestyle; I felt like I was ready to pick the profession.

So in the spring of 1997, I flew out to Los Angeles for my rabbinical school interview. I was accepted, and in July of 1997, my supervisor at Leo Burnett sent a memo to his superiors: "We've lost Daniel to a higher calling! In two weeks, he will leave us to study to become a rabbi. We wish him well and will miss him."

In 2002, five and a half years after Jay's funeral, I was ordained as a rabbi. His death remained an unanswered question, but as I stood on the stage and was called "Rabbi" for the first time, I closed my eyes and said quietly to myself, "thank you, Jay." I would have given anything for him to be alive, but his death gave me a gift. It forced me to confront the question of my life's meaning at a young age and spurred me forward to live purposefully rather than just coasting along. Jay wasn't a religious guy, but I think he would have appreciated the decisions I'd made. The last person in our class received his ordination certificate. The dean announced to the audience, "Distinguished rabbis and friends, I am proud to present to you the world's newest rabbis!" As the crowd erupted with applause, I closed my eyes again and said, "This is for you, Jay. I miss you."

After ordination, I started my first job as the Executive Director of Camp Ramah in California. Ramah is a network of seven overnight summer camps and three day camps across North America. At the same time, I also dreamed of writing a book. Like many young rabbis, I thought I would one day publish my spiritual Jewish journey, about how I discovered the value of Shabbat and keeping kosher. I imagined I would write my own modern, compelling explanations of the Jewish holidays and prayer and our textual tradition. I would make the argument to my generation of Jews for why being Jewish is hip, fun, and existentially important. That was the book I thought I was supposed to write. I would give anything to have written that book instead, but it is not the book God had in mind for me.

chapter 3

Joel

Now cracks a noble heart. Good night, sweet prince
And flights of angels sing thee to thy rest.
—SHAKESPEARE

1

Coming to Camp

THE RAMAH BOARD WELCOMES me as rabbi of the camp. They are wonderful people. It is a great job. The first few years are hectic but they go well. Camp Ramah serves nearly 8,000 campers and staff each summer. Approximately 1,300 campers from across the Western region of the United States spend either two or four weeks every summer at our Ramah camp in Ojai, California. While there, they enjoy all the fun activities of a traditional camp—art, swimming, sports, hiking, dance—and also engage in learning the Hebrew language, traditional Jewish prayer, study and practice. Our Ramah also functions as a year-round conference center through which we run our own winter weekends and programs. In addition, we rent out the camp for synagogues and other groups to run their own programs. Each summer, we need to hire more than 250 staff members to serve as counselors and specialists.

A few years into the job, our longtime music specialist cannot return for the 2005 summer and we need someone to run our music program. I hear through the grapevine that someone from Dallas named Joel was recently admitted to rabbinical school and, good news, he is a guitar-playing Pied Piper for kids. So I pick up the phone and try to sell him on Ramah. I convince his wife, Heather, that camp will be a great way to transition to Los Angeles and rabbinical school. "You can live at camp over the summer," I tell them over the phone, "and, on days off, you can search for an apartment. You'll meet lots of people from the LA Jewish community, and what better place for your three boys? They're really close in age to our own boys—it'll be great!" They say yes. I sigh with relief, and move on to fill another staff position.

Summer arrives. Joel wears a tie-dyed shirt and carries a guitar most places around camp. Heather is laid back and funny. In the whirl of controlled chaos that is camp each summer, our families became friends. Joel and Heather's oldest son, Coleman, is six and our eldest, Alon, is just a few months shy of his sixth birthday; their middle son, Miles, is four and our middle son, Benjamin, is nearly four too; their youngest, Ellis, is a baby and Jennifer is pregnant with our third child. The boys play at our cottage. Heather and Jennifer go on walks and joke about potty training. Rushing from here to there, I stop and watch Joel teach campers our traditional camp songs as if he's gone to Ramah for years and sung them all his life. On Shabbat mornings, Joel starts a service for the three to six-year-olds and their parents. My children fall in love with his songs and gentleness.

I did not grow up at Ramah and, despite being the director, I often feel like an outsider. Camp veterans tend to cling to their own, not out of hostility or suspicion, but because they've known each other for so long, been through so much, and treasure the precious few weeks they have together at camp each summer. After a few summers, I am accepted, even appreciated. Gradually, my wife and I form friendships with the veteran camp staff, but our bond with Joel and his family feels different. They are newcomers like us.

Joel doesn't just fit in to camp; he makes an impression. Ask anyone and they'll tell you Joel is not just talented; he is a *mensch*, a kind and humble person. He is sweet and gentle and selfless and giving. Joel does not speak badly about anyone; he lacks that sense of destructive competition that so often ruins relationships. Joel isn't just a good Jew, he is a good person.

It's midnight one evening when Joel comes over to the director's cottage. Even at midnight, it is not easy for me to sleep most nights at

Ramah. Not that the phone rings so often in the middle of the night. A few times my pager will go off. During the summer I clip an emergency pager to my belt for parents who must reach me immediately or, when an ambulance is called to the camp, the *merpa'ah*—the infirmary—will page me. When that happens there are long, alarming beeps and I look down and see "911" on the screen. For many weeks after the summer, I find myself feeling around the side of my belt for the pager, checking to be sure it's there long after the kids have gone home, like an amputee feeling for a missing limb. So I worry. I wonder if all the kids are sleeping.

Tonight, Joel keeps me company. We drink some tea and talk on the porch. I tell him about what happened today. An eighth-grade girl cut herself. Not by accident. On purpose. With a knife. It's a thing now with adolescents: cutting. Psychologists explain that girls are hurting so much inside that they cut themselves, not to commit suicide but to external-ize the pain. We sent her home, not as a punishment, but because our 18-year-old counselors are not equipped to help her. Her friends are not equipped to help her. I am not equipped to help her. I point to a patch of grass near the porch and tell Joel I've named it "the crying grass." The crying grass is where the girl who cut herself and her friends cried and cried and said good-bye to each other before she went home, God willing, to get help and become healthy again. I tell Joel how I tried to fall asleep a few hours ago but when I closed my eyes, I saw the girl's eyes filled with so much pain that she drew a knife across her skin to let the darkness ooze out. I couldn't stop thinking of her tears.

Joel reaches out a hand. "You're doing good, Daniel. I love Ramah. It is a great place, not just for me, but for the Jewish people, for the world. You're doing lots of good, Daniel." He reminds me how lucky I am. How Ramah is a place where thousands of young kids fall in love with Jewish life. How they meet other Jewish kids from different communities and feel a sense of connection to one another, to the Jewish tradition. Joel helps me feel lucky again; not just because I am living my life well. I am lucky to have a best friend again, like Jay.

Our friendship deepens. Our families grow closer. After the sum-mer, Joel enrolls in a class I teach fall semester at the rabbinical school on the history, theology, and law of Jewish prayer. He is a good student. I enjoy reading his papers and getting to be closer to his experience in rabbinical school.

Our families spend the 2006 summer together at camp again. Joel and I take the boys to the tree house, and sleep out overnight on our own private father-son camping trips. He plays guitar for the boys, and, in the morning, we drive to town and buy them hot chocolate while we enjoy coffee and bring lattes back to camp for our wives. During the year, we get together most Sunday afternoons. Their three boys play with our three boys. Sometimes the four adults talk together, but just as often, Jen and Heather spend time together as Joel and I get to catch up on things. We talk about school and fatherhood. Joel plays piano, and I sing along. He is the kind of friend I want to have my whole life.

2

January 2007

Joel and his family are at Ramah with their synagogue for a winter weekend retreat. I don't bring my family to camp for every synagogue rental, or we'd spend nearly every weekend driving back and forth, never at home. But we go this time and enjoy the chance to spend a whole Shabbat with Joel and his family. Our boys run freely. They form a secret club. In the large drainage pipe under the road between the dining hall and the tent area, they create a private fort for meetings and battles against imaginary enemies of all that is right and good in the world. They swoop into meals for a few minutes, gobble up food, say hi (or not), and run back out to play.

Jennifer and Heather, Joel and I enjoy the chance to be together while the children play safely without us. Joel leads a kids' service the next morning. He leads singing on his guitar on Saturday night. I enjoy the chance to be at camp with no responsibilities for the program. The weather is chilly and cloudy—winter in California, but balmy compared to the rest of the country. Throughout the weekend, a few of us notice Joel seems tired and pale, almost gray. We think he's coming down with a cold.

I am at work on Monday when the phone rings. It is Heather. "Daniel, I'm at Cedars-Sinai. Joel still wasn't feeling well, so we finally came in. They are admitting him. They think he has cancer." I don't cry. I don't gasp. I forget whatever emails I need to write, phone calls I need to make, meetings I need to be at. "Heather, I'm coming. I'm going to call Jen. I'll be there in half an hour," I say. I close my computer, put it in my bag, tell someone in my office that a friend is in the hospital, that I have to go, and I walk out.

When I arrive at Cedars, Joel is somewhere getting tested. I give Heather a long hug and tell her, "It's going to be okay." For a moment, I think back to Jay and his long battle with leukemia. I squeeze Heather a little tighter and whisper in her ear, "This is a very good hospital. It'll be alright," I say, praying I am right this time, but wondering to myself, "How can this be happening again?"

3

April 2007

Ramah runs a Passover program. Our camp in the Ojai valley is a beautiful place to retreat from the world and celebrate the coming of spring. Plus, a lot of people love that we do the cleaning for them—the intense purge, mandated by Jewish law for the holiday, that rids the home of every speck of leavened bread. So, each April, a group of forty or fifty families comes to camp and spends Passover together, eating, learning, praying, eating, playing sports, eating, swimming and, did I mention, eating?

After the 2005 summer, I hired Heather to run our Passover program. I figured that, with Joel in school, they needed some income. I knew Heather used to work at Texas Instruments, and saw that she is organized, friendly, and has a good head for business and logistics—all important skills for running a program. I figured too that Joel could help lead the Seders and prayers.

When Heather accepted the job as director of Passover Camp, perhaps the most important thing for me was that it meant our families could spend eight full days in the same place, away from our hectic lives in the city, together. Passover 2006 went great—the camp was full. Our families sat together at the same table, went on hikes, and everyone enjoyed a wonderful holiday together. I told Heather she was hired for as many Passovers as we could keep her. When Joel got sick, we found a replacement for Heather as Passover director, but stressed that they were more than welcome to come and spend as much of the holiday at Ramah as they could.

The holiday begins. Joel has already started his treatments and being up at camp is not the easiest environment for him. He needs to take it easy and keep his distance from the crowds of people to minimize the risk of infection. We sit together at the Seder. We eat bitter herbs, dip parsley in salt water. As people around the room take turns reading the story, I think about how Passover is a holiday that celebrates God's saving power. God enters history and takes the Jewish people out of their slavery in Egypt.

Passover is the defining story of the Jewish tradition. Every day Jews recall the Exodus just before we petition God in personal prayer. We say, "Blessed are You Adonai who redeemed Israel," as if to say, "Adonai—God—You entered history before. You answered us when we cried out and saved us from slavery. Please hear our prayers and answer us, too!" As the story comes to an end and we prepare to eat the matzah, I think to myself how, this Passover, our prayers definitely need answering.

At services the next morning, we chant *Hallel*, songs of praise to God. I remember how, years before in Jerusalem, I sang *Hallel* and understood the words I was singing for the first time: "The dead cannot not praise You, nor those who go down in silence. But we shall praise You, now and forevermore, Hallelujah!" (Psalm 115:17). Years before in Jerusalem, I sang "The dead cannot praise You," thought of my dying friend Jay, and started to cry during the prayers. It was one of my first meaningful experiences with the Jewish liturgy. Saying the words of the psalmist stirred an emotion within me, gave voice to a feeling deep inside. It connected my tears to generations of Jews before and helped me feel not so alone. It also gave a sense of depth to the sadness I felt.

This morning, as we arrive to Psalm 115—it is sung to a triumphant, marching band kind of melody—I notice Joel belting out the psalm while his youngest son, Ellis, sits on a bench looking up to him. Joel looks over at me. Our eyes meet for a moment. I look down at Joel's son and think of Jay. I am filled with fear. I face the ark and push through the melody. I sing to be strong for Joel. He and his family stay for four days, half the holiday, but Joel is feeling weak and needs to return home. He spends the second half of the eight-day festival in the hospital undergoing more treatments.

On the last day of Passover, I give a sermon and lead the *Yizkor* memorial service in which we remember our loved ones who have passed away—"Yizkor" from the first word of the prayer, meaning "May God remember." After a few introductory words, there are private prayers for the seven relatives. At the end, before the prayers for martyrs in Jewish history and those who died in the *Shoah* (the Hebrew for "Holocaust"), there is a prayer for friends and others. I remember Jay. For a moment, I think of Joel. It feels like bad luck, like I might accidentally curse his recovery by thinking of him during a memorial prayer. So I close the prayer book and look away. I try to think of anything else until everyone is ready for the service to continue.

4

May 2007

It is *Yom HaShoah*—Holocaust Remembrance Day—and I am at a conference in Israel. I lead the morning prayers and, as part of the repetition of the *Amidah* (literally the "standing prayer," it refers to the central prayer of the Jewish liturgy), I include a special paragraph marking *Yom HaShoah*. Such an inclusion in the fixed set of prayers is a liturgically important statement. It says that we officially recognize this day as one to remember before God, a terrible tragedy in Jewish history when we experienced the possibility of God's absence from history (the paradox of talking to God about God's absence, all the while ignoring the possibility of God's continued absence, would be funny were it not so terrifying). Such an addition to the liturgy might go unnoticed in an American Jewish community unless the rabbi called attention to it, but in Israel, where everyone understands the words of the Hebrew prayers as they are said, nobody misses the change.

Passover celebrates God's saving power in history. The *Shoah* represents the ultimate moment in Jewish history when God did not save His people. Jews who prayed for salvation were murdered in the Holocaust. Maybe God has the power but it wasn't His job to save? But isn't there a point when a good God must help because, if He doesn't, He can't be good? And if God won't help, why ask? We beg God to save us. We pray for healing. But if He doesn't help, someone tells us not to blame God.

I think about these things as the services continue. Over breakfast, I think about how, in the very same *Amidah* in which I religiously acknowledged a moment of God's absence in history, I also prayed to God to heal Joel. I slowly sip my coffee and wonder some more about the prayer I said.

5

August 2007

It is a much longer, more complicated road than we thought it would be. Joel has leukemia, but it is a very rare form, resistant to normal treatments. Fortunately, one of the best places in the world to treat it is City of Hope hospital, in Duarte, California, a 45-minute drive from West Los Angeles. One of the best leukemia doctors in the world, Dr. Stephen Forman, is there. Heather fights with the insurance company and wins; Joel is transferred there. A donor to Camp Ramah is also a big donor at City of Hope. I make a call, the donor makes a call, Joel is accepted as Dr. Forman's patient. Concerts are held. Money is raised. There is a bone marrow drive; a pretty good match is found. Joel has a transplant over the summer. It is preceded by a brutal radiation regime to kill all the cancer cells, and it kills many healthy ones too. It is a descent into hell, but one we all assume is a prelude to a re-emergence back to strength, recovery, and a happy ending.

I am busy. Running camp is always overwhelming. I call Joel a few times, but it is hard for him to talk, and hard for me to catch him at a time when his energy is high. Weeks go by. Groups of campers and staff and his classmates visit Joel. They put on gloves and masks and gowns, they deliver dozens of cards; sometimes someone brings a guitar. If Joel is up to it, he plays, and they sing. Beneath his mask, Joel tries to smile and put them at ease.

Finally, I carve out a few hours to leave camp and make the drive 70 miles from Ramah to City of Hope. I turn off my cell phone and the radio. As the car winds its way from the mountains towards the coast, I feel like I am playing a role in a film I've seen before. This is not the first time a best friend of mine has battled leukemia. But I am not going to leave for Israel this time, not going off to find myself. This time, I'm going to be there for my friend. I'm going to help get him through.

6

Blind Faith

As the traffic moves along and my eyes strain against the mid-afternoon sun, my thoughts return to Jay. It wasn't fair when, during the summer after high school, as the rest of us prepared to go away to college for the first time, Jay had to defer acceptance to Northwestern University because he'd come out of remission. Fortunately, after some chemotherapy in the summer and fall, he was in remission again, and went off to start the winter semester. But a few years later, when Jay and I roomed together at Northwestern, he dropped out of remission one more time and, in a matter of days, his room in our apartment on Maple Avenue was empty. I remember the summer he had the bone marrow transplant, the radiation knocked him down until he had to throw up; they stood him up again and it continued. This went on for days.

In the last years of his life, Jay wrote a poem about faith and God. As a rabbi, it keeps me honest in whatever belief I have; it is a poem to which I must answer, a constant reminder that faith is never easy if it is true and real, that faith, when it is given to us, should never be blind. "Blind Faith," was written by Jay A. Rosen on April 23rd, 1996, eight months before he died.

Blind Faith

I lie awake in bed and dream about the days,
Days of skipping, days of jumping,
carefree days I thought were meant to last.
Now the nights go on forever, an eternity in the dark,
Football fields and late-night romps, fading memories from the past.

Let us adore the ever-living God,
But where did He go?
Let us adore the ever-living God,
Please tell me why it is so.

Once upon a long ago, when the hours were flying by,
I wished for more, so many games to be played.
But the fairy tale is over and the big bad wolf is bolder,
Just get me through another day.

Let us adore the ever-living God,
But where is He now?
Let us adore the ever-living God,
For whom we take our vows.

Speak to me of destiny, speak to me of a test,
Of Abraham and his sacrifice, of David at his best.
Now gone is the faith to everything there is a season,
Gone is the faith that behind suffering, a reason.

Let us adore the ever-living God,
Hang the mezuzah on the door.
Recite like robots the words we're told,
But I no longer know what for.

Let us adore . . .

7

City of Hope

I meet Avi and Warren, friends of Joel's from rabbinical school, at the front of the building, and we walk up together with a sense of confidence, of mission, even excitement to see him, not only because he is our friend, but because visiting feels part of a great effort, "Joel's recovery."

I sit at the foot of the bed as Joel talks slowly, as if using the muscles of his face takes great effort. Joel weighs 125 pounds and says that he looks "like someone from Cambodia." He is yellow from a bout with hepatitis, one of many illnesses that have attacked his organs over the summer. He struggles to stand for five seconds, or to sit in a chair or bed. The three of us visit with him for an hour or so, alternating between talking about sports and talking about his condition, encouraging him by saying that he will walk out of this hospital one day soon.

Our metaphors—things we might say in other situations, like "you're in the fourth quarter," or "there's a light at the end of the tunnel"—fall flat and sound stupid and inadequate. We are smart enough to know that we don't know what to say—that there is nothing to be said—yet we know that our being there itself means a lot.

The TV is on mute, tuned to a game. I joke about many guys being jealous, what with football season starting soon and his having nothing to do except sit in front of a TV. But football games don't matter much when you have to work to stand up. They are a diversion, one not even so welcome these days. An air of helplessness fills the room, deflates our altruistic enthusiasm in visiting. I feel a measure of relief when a therapist walks in and asks if Joel has time for his exercises. We all understand the priority; Joel has to take every opportunity to jumpstart his body back to health and strength. "I'm kicking you guys outta here now," he says.

We stand up, and I say "All right, my friend." I take an awkward leap and suggest a prayer. "Let's do a *mi'sheberach* before we go." Joel nods his head slowly; he is allowing me to say a prayer for the sick. Not wanting to increase the chance of infection, I ask Joel if I can hold his hand, and he agrees. My gloved right hand holds his left and I reach with my left hand to Avi sitting next to me. Avi and Warren join hands and Warren holds Joel's right on the other side of the bed, so we form a circle of prayer. I look Joel in the eye and try to reach out to him from beneath my mask, to tell him without words that I love him, very much; that I don't want to leave my sick friend like I did years before; that I want to drop my life and ignore my wife and kids and sit at his bedside, but I cannot. His eyes say he understands and loves me, too. I close my eyes and speak, slowly, the ancient prayer.

> *Me'sheberach avoteinu, Avraham, Yitzchak, v'Ya'akov, Sarah, Rivkah, Rachel, v'Leah...*May the One who blessed our ancestors, Abraham, Isaac, and Jacob, Sarah, Rebecca, Rachel, and Leah, may He bless and heal the one who is sick, Joel, the son of Sarah Miriam. May the Holy Blessing One pour compassion upon him to strengthen him and heal him and send him soon a complete healing to all his organs and limbs, a healing of body, a healing of soul, amongst all the sick of Israel, speedily soon. Amen.

Where am I as these words leave my mouth? I am standing next to Joel's bed, wearing rubber gloves, feeling Joel's hand weakly grasp mine. I am a coward, hiding a true prayer behind someone else's words. I lack courage to confront my own fear and speak words of my own. Yet, I am also grateful for the prayer—old, ancient words, Hebrew words that feel laden with power, spoken for centuries by worried mothers, brothers, cousins. But Hebrew words are not magic. They will not bring a cure, like coins you put into a vending machine to receive candy. And yet, I say them anyway, just in case that's actually how it works.

The words of the prayer flash through my mind.

"Son of Sarah Miriam," for the mother is the source of compassion and healing, of the breast that suckles a baby. She feels the illness of her son in her bosom and is connected to wellsprings in a way a man is not. Joel's mother died long ago; how will she help him now? May her memory and righteous deeds, may her loving soul watching over him, give him strength. I do not know if I agree with a theology that asserts that she can help, but I don't care. You don't pray according to a theological system.

"All his organs and limbs" is a strange phrase. Not poetic, but real. Hospital rooms aren't poetic; they're harsh, fluorescent. They're where you go when your liver doesn't work. Body parts. His liver is broken. He's yellow. We're not messing around with ideas now, God. This hospital, this prayer: heal his organs and limbs.

I say "a healing of soul" with yearning in my heart. Joel is broken. He needs hope and light, and he needs beyond what he can summon from himself. He needs strength and healing from somewhere else, from You. Please.

"Amongst all the sick of Israel"? I don't want to think about everybody else! Joel is 37. He has a wife and three children. He is studying to be a rabbi, for God's sake. To serve You, damn it! And yet others are sick. Joel is a selfless guy; he'd be the first to tell me he's not the only one. Even from a hospital bed, he's a healer; he's healing me. Heal him. Heal them all. Please.

Amen.

I open my eyes and look at him again. A tear is in his eyes, and I feel one in mine. The physical therapist moves toward the bed, and I let go of Joel's hand and turn away. We leave the room and walk down the sterile, quiet hallways in silence. I don't mention to Avi and Warren how I used to visit Jay when he was sick. We leave the hospital. Outside is another day of Southern California sunshine. The radiation and the transplant are a prelude, but I fear it is not the sort we hope for.

8

Friday, November 16, 2007

Autumn is filled with infections and recoveries for Joel. Middle-of-the-night trips to the hospital, triumphant homecomings. But then I wake up on Friday morning and Jennifer reads me Heather's blog from Joel's Care Page[1].

> We Need Your Prayers Tonight
>
> The doctors just called me (it's 8:30 PM Thursday night) and they are moving Joel to the Intensive Care Unit. He has developed a serious infection and his body is struggling to fight it. He has a fever, nausea and stomach pain. He tested positive for the c-diff bacteria again, and the doctor is concerned that it may have moved into his bloodstream. Since this is the third time he's had this infection, they also believe he has a resistant form. His blood pressure is very low and his breathing is labored. His bowels are not moving so it is difficult to get the antibiotics to the site of the infection. They may have to do some serious interventions over the next 24 hours such as ventilators, etc.
>
> I spent the day with him and could see that he is very sick. The doctor called and told me that I should come back in tonight. My nanny is staying the night with the boys.
>
> Please pray and pray and pray. This is a serious fight.

I walk into City of Hope and tell the man at the visitor's desk I need the room number for Joel Shickman and that I am looking for his wife, Heather. Without looking down at a list he says, "Oh, yes, Joel moved to the ICU. Room 3209. It's such a shame; we're all thinking about him. I think Heather is in the Bistro getting some breakfast."

City of Hope is a huge hospital. I am struck that the guy manning a visitor's desk for a hospital tower with hundreds of patients calls Joel by his first name, knows his situation had changed, and knows that his wife had gone to breakfast. It is a testament to the place and to how many people must have visited him during his stay. It is also a sign of how damn long Joel has been coming here.

I walk up to the third floor, look around the lobby; Heather is not there. I pick up the phone next to the ICU entrance and listen to it ring

---

1. Care Pages websites are free patient blogs that connect friends and family during a health challenge. To find out more, go to www.carepages.com.

the nurses' station. A nurse answers, and the door clicks to unlock. I pull it open and walk cautiously through a first set of doors into a room that divides the ICU from the lobby. It is a sort of antechamber that, in addition to increasing sterility in the area beyond, gives the visitor a sense of entering a separate, holy place, like the inner chamber of God's holy Temple.

I pull open the second set of doors, walk through, and hear them click behind me. I step slowly and quietly, trying to respect the seriousness of what happens in an ICU, of machines and fluids and beeping monitors, of tears and prayers. I follow the numbers on the rooms, looking cautiously at the surroundings. There is a bald young child in the first room. In another, a TV is playing and a teenage girl sits on her bed playing board games amidst the IV lines. A few rooms beyond is a young man who, from the bandages and casts, I figure was in a car accident. At the end of the hall lies an elderly man, unconscious.

To my left is room 3209. I stop and gaze in from 20 feet away. Joel wears a headband under his chin and above his forehead to keep in place a respirator. He is blue and pale and yellowish green all at once, and he is unconscious. I stand still for a few moments longer, then slowly step backwards, turn around, and decide to find Heather first before visiting more. . .if what I've done can be described as a visit. I am afraid of what I see and rationalize to myself that it is more important to check on Heather and learn more about how the doctors plan to get Joel out of there.

I retreat to the main floor, where I ask the same man if he's seen Heather. While I'm asking, I see her across the lobby, coming from the direction of the Bistro. She's been here all night and wanted a real breakfast, not just a sandwich, so she ate where they serve real eggs. We hug for a long time, one of those hugs in which you try to tell the person, "You're not alone. I'm not going to let you be alone. I'm here for you. I'm so, so sad, but I love you so much. We're going to be okay," even though you're hugging because things are not okay, and it's clear things will not be okay, and may never be again. We take the elevator upstairs and sit down to talk in the lobby outside the ICU.

The lobbies of City of Hope are beautiful. On every floor of the Helford Building, where Joel has been treated the past six months, are tall, wide windows. They look beyond other buildings in the complex, to the green, tree-covered San Gabriel mountains. The windows flood the lobbies with natural, healing light. When patients are healthy enough to venture out of their rooms, they have a view of the world that awaits them. When patients are too sick to visit the lobby, as Joel was so much of the time, or when patients can't open their eyes, as Joel could not this morning; then it is the patients' loved ones who sit anxiously beneath the tall, wide windows bright with hope.

Doctors stop by and tell us about infections and medicines, treatments and specialists, and the team of people working to help Joel. We return to our conversation. Some phone calls we ignore, others we answer. A friend comes with snacks and hugs, and we talk some more. Heather visits with Joel alone and returns after a while. The conversations continue. Later, a nurse practitioner comes by and tells us many of the same details the doctors did. Joel has two infections, one a c-diff infection that has returned for the third time. The c-diff will be difficult to treat this time, having survived antibiotics the first two times around. He is in septic shock. His kidneys are weak, and he was given a lot of fluids yesterday to flush out his system. His blood pressure is low.

She answers questions and gives clear explanations of what is happening. At the end, she looks at Heather and says, "We're working hard and throwing a lot at him. And people do survive this. But he may not. I want you to have hope, but I don't want you to be surprised if he doesn't make it. You need to prepare yourself for this. And you need to prepare the kids. You should bring them to see him soon."

The words hang in the air. We look at Heather, whose gaze stays fixed on her. The nurse practitioner speaks a bit more; we thank her for her honesty, and she leaves. Standing in a lobby beneath bright, wide windows, we cry and cry, and hug some more.

9

Preparing for Shabbat

Plans are made to bring Coleman and Miles and Ellis to the hospital later tonight. I leave that afternoon for a few hours and drive 45 minutes back to West Los Angeles. I collect clothes, a *tallit*, a *siddur*, and other things I will need to spend Shabbat in the hospital. Shabbat lasts 25 hours, from 18 minutes before sunset Friday night to 42 minutes after sunset Saturday night, when three stars are visible in the sky. I take a set of portable candlesticks, forgetting that one cannot light fire, for any reason, anywhere in a hospital.

Reb Mimi Feigelson is an orthodox rabbi. She chose the title "Reb" versus "Rabbi" out of respect to the Hasidic and Orthodox communities she's aligned with. Most importantly, she's my teacher and friend. Reb Mimi brings food for Shabbat to my house. Inside two large paper grocery bags is enough chicken and salad and chocolate *rugalach* rolls for me and Heather's family, plates and napkins, plastic ware, cups, and a bottle of kosher grape juice for *Kiddush* (the sanctification of Shabbat, said over wine or grape juice). Also included are six small, whole challah rolls so that, at each meal—Friday dinner, Saturday lunch, and *seuda shlishit* (the Sabbath third meal)—we can have *lechem mishneh*, two loaves of bread, as a reminder of the double portion of *manna* God gave to the Jewish people in the desert and a reminder that, on Shabbat, we should rest and experience God's abundance and goodness.

Shabbat is supposed to be a taste of the World to Come, of what the world will be like when suffering and pain will disappear and all will be made right. Before I start the car for the long return to the hospital, I grab my rabbi's manual that has within it prayers for many occasions, among them the *vidui*, the confession that one says on one's deathbed or, if a person is too sick to say it for himself, that another person should say for him.

Traffic crawls. When it stops altogether, I read emails on my Blackberry that have been pouring in all day. One of them is from Joel's friend, Noam Raucher, a rabbinical student. He emailed the Ziegler community from Israel asking this Shabbat that when we sing Shalom Aleichem (a prayer in which we welcome angels to our Shabbat table), we replace the final verse *tzeitchem l'shalom*—leave in peace—with *shivtichem b'shalom*—meaning "sit in peace." Noam asks us to invite the angels to sit, to stay a while, to dwell with us, and most importantly, to dwell with Joel this Shabbat, to bring him peace and healing and God's loving light.

On the road, I listen to a recording of a concert of Rabbi Shlomo Carlebach, a Hasidic *rebbe* and master, and a composer known popularly as "The Singing Rabbi." One song repeats a verse from Psalm 126, a psalm traditional Jews sing on Shabbat and festivals before the grace after meals. The verse is *hazor'im b'dim'ah, b'rina yiktzoru*,—"those who sow in tears, they will reap in joy." Reb Shlomo, as he was affectionately called by his followers, explains how some Jews re-read the verse to reveal a secret of life, of being real: everything we do in this life, we must do "with tears and with joy."

But when he sings the verse in the song, he repeats, "those who sow in tears, in tears, in tears, those who sow in tears, in tears, in tears, those who sow in tears, in tears, in tears," and only at the end does he say, "they will reap in joy." I drive east, the sun descends on the horizon behind me and I sing "in tears," again and again with Reb Shlomo. Joy feels very far away.

10

Shabbat—Friday Evening

I return to the hospital minutes before sunset as Shabbat begins, drop off the food and clothes at the entrance to Joel's building, park the car, make a few trips to bring everything up to the 3rd floor and get settled in. When I arrive, Heather is sitting with a hospital social worker who has a picture book of the ICU; pictures of the door with the phone next to it that you use to call the nurses to let you in; pictures of the anteroom that made me feel like I was entering the Holy of Holies, the inner chamber of the Temple; pictures of medicine cabinets and machines, of IV tubes and a dialysis machine, of a respirator and a mask and a strap to hold them in place; and two pictures of Joel she had taken with a digital camera earlier that morning. One picture is from farther away; the second is from closer up. The pictures are to show the kids and help prepare them to see their dad, to see him in a strange place with scary things happening to him.

I am struck with gratitude that there is a social worker who has this book, that somebody thought to create it, to give her a digital camera and a photo printer, to pay her to be here with this book and to help explain all of this to Joel's little children, because it is utterly ridiculous to think that the best parent on the planet would be able to make that book, or any book, or take and print out these pictures, or any picture, for her kids, while her husband (or his wife) lies unconscious in the ICU. Of course nobody could ever do that for him or herself. "How terrible this moment is," I think. "Yet how wonderful is this holy social worker."

I am grateful that when the kids arrive in a little while, when they hug their mom and sit down to a dinner of grape juice and challah and chicken and salads and chocolate *rugalach*, and then, with their tummies full, when they ask to see their dad, there will be a holy picture book made by the holy social worker who will speak holy words in a calm voice. Her book of pictures will help their dad, my friend, seem less scary.

After their visit, the nanny and the boys go home for the night. We walk them to the minivan, get them settled in, and Coleman starts to cry.

"Why do you have to stay at the hospital again? Please. Please come home with us, Mom! Please."

I don't know where Heather's strength comes from in this moment. I don't know how you hear your children plead with you to come home because they need you, and of course, you need them and love them and want to be there for them just to hold their own breaking hearts. I don't know where her strength comes from as she says goodbye for the night to her kids. Where does her strength come from to watch the minivan drive away, to walk with me back to the ICU, to stand at the bedside of their father, and to stroke Joel's hair and caress his chest as it rises and falls from the ventilator that keeps him alive? That is all I can say about God in this moment. I do not know where Heather's strength comes from, for a shudder of despair fills my own heart and I have only tears.

On the way up from the parking lot, I say to Heather, "I believe we're going to get through this and that it won't come to it, but if it does, there is something called the *vidui*."

"Last rites?" she asks.

"Sort of. It is a confession, a deathbed confession, to help us leave this world forgiven." It feels inadequate, but I try to explain how the prayer begins with a cry for healing. "May it be Your will that You send perfect healing" to the one who is sick, and only then does the prayer continue, "Yet if it be your final decree that he be taken by death…" I try to explain that the saying of this prayer is not an act of despair.

"How do you know when it's time to say it?"

"I think we ask the nurses. They have a sense of these things."

She tells me I should do it if the time comes.

From nine o'clock on, we hold vigil in room 3209 as Joel Shickman fights to stay in this world. People around the globe pray for Joel this Shabbat. The world revolves on its axis from Jerusalem to New York and, as Shabbat arrives to Los Angeles, I join thousands of Jews and sing "Shalom Aleichem," but, as Noam requested, I do not bid the angels "*tzeitchem l'shalom*—"leave in peace." I bid them to stay, "sit in peace!" Bring Shabbat to room 3209, to heal! To heal.

Time passes.

Heather sees my copy of the rabbi's manual. "Not yet," she says.

"No. Not yet," I say, and I put the manual on a chair at the back of the room. She is right.

Joel had asked for "all measures" to be taken to save him. It is painful for us now to witness his struggle prolonged, perhaps beyond any hope for healing, but Joel had faith. His faith was not a flat caricature; in my conversations with him during the course of his illness, Joel gave voice to his anger and bewilderment at God and why this was happening to him. But he wanted every measure to be taken because he believed that, until the very last moment, healing could be at hand. "It is Joel's death," Heather says to me. Joel believed in God's saving power, in God's everlasting grace.

I say *tehillim*, psalms, and sing *nigunim*, wordless melodies. At Joel's bedside I pray in sacred words and yearning melodies. I hope rhythms and songs of our people will not just set the mood. I call upon the depth within these pleas to summon the merit of our ancestors, of holy ones who came before, who died and sanctified God's name and praised God with these very sounds. I summon them all to Joel's side, to plead for his life, for healing. I pray for a *nes*—a miracle—something that people see and, when they hear about it or see it or experience it, they acknowledge God. If Joel gets better, how many will give thanks to God for Joel's life! Not for my own sake, though I want Joel to be better so much; nor even for Joel's sake, though he would give anything to fight and scratch for just one more moment, but I pray for a *nes* that Joel should be healed and God's name will be sanctified.

> Heal him God, for thousands of people stand vigil this night. They love Joel and have followed his story. Jewish children in communities throughout the entire Western U.S. have learned Your songs from Joel. Hundreds, maybe thousands of people, have followed Joel's story on the Internet. How great and holy a miracle it will be! In this age of darkness and confusion, how many people will praise You and know You if You only will heal him! So he can be a rabbi, a teacher of Your holy Torah! And what Torah he will teach! A sweet and gentle and good and pure and true Torah because of his great love for You. Heal him. He is a great light in Your world. Heal him and let him shine Your light! Heal him. Heal him. May the words of my mouth be acceptable to You, my Rock and my Redeemer,

and may the One who makes peace in the heavens make peace
upon us, and all the people Israel, and let us say, Amen.

We sing and pray and, as we do, amidst us are messengers from
God—nurses who are kind and gentle, changing bags and adjusting the
symphony of machines; ICU nurses who too often see death but never
fail to care for Joel and for us. Jewish tradition teaches that the angels who
surround God in heaven have appointed times, when they come, watch,
and then depart again. The ICU nurses remind me of the angels and their
shifts in heaven. They have appointed times to keep watch, to come and
go, to earn our gratitude.

During a song, one of the nurses calls Heather to speak with the
doctor on the phone. Heather leaves and is gone for some time. When
the song I am singing ends, I find her standing at the counter, facing away
with the phone in her hand. I place my hand on her shoulder; she puts the
phone down, and turns to me. Tears run down her cheeks. "The doctor
said it's not working. The treatments they are trying are not working."
We hug and cry and cry. Heather's mom, Paula, comes to us, and I tell
her, "The doctor says the treatments are not working." We hold Heather
between us and there are tears, only tears.

The machines beep and hum. Joel's blood pressure and heart rate
fluctuate and set off alarms that continue to go off while we sit with him.
I take breaks, go to the bathroom, get coffee, walk the lobby. Paula takes
breaks. Heather takes very few. Somehow, she stands at Joel's side for
hours, kisses his forehead and whispers to him in his ears; touches his
chest and arms to tell him, "I am here. I love you. You are not alone."
Joel's blood pressure continues to fall. He gets sodium bicarbonate and it
rises again, but his body is not processing enough oxygen and remains in
septic shock. The nurses explain what they are doing, but when we ask,
each of them says, "It is not looking good." When one of the nurses leaves
the room with these words hanging in the air, Heather looks at me and
says, "Ask."

I leave Joel's room reluctant to admit the possibility of his death and,
at the same time, with a sense of duty to do the *vidui* for him. I think about
this sense of duty to "do the *vidui*." Why did I bring my rabbi's manual?
Why did I make sure to tell Heather about this moment? I wonder about
the purity of my ego and where my sense of duty comes from. I wonder
why I wanted to become a rabbi so long ago. Was it from a real desire to

serve God? Or do I find meaning in the rituals of religious life because they place me at the center? Idolatry of the self is a constant fear of mine, a special danger for those who presume to serve God.

Once, I thought that a person who dares to do something so holy as saying *vidui* for someone else, that person in that moment must be able to discern if he serves his own ego, or God. Now I'm not so sure. I am filled with doubt about myself, about the purity of my religious intentions. I realize I do not even know myself. All I can I do is pray to be pure.

I walk to the area of the nurses' station and explain that there is a religious rite that should be performed shortly before a person's death. I ask if she has a sense of whether that is imminent. I figure an ICU nurse will know, will have a sense of what is ahead. "It's really hard to tell. I don't know what to tell you," she says . . . of course. Of course, because I see now that nobody really knows.

I return to the room and take my place again at Joel's side. I ask Heather what song Joel would like to hear. She says something that I don't expect.

"Sloop John B."

I want to be helpful. I want to help sing it but confess, "I don't know the words." So over the pulse of the respirator and the buzz of pumps and monitors and through a web of cords, Heather sings to her soul mate who lies dying a song about going home, just going home.

I have said the *vidui* for a person only once, for my grandma Lillian almost ten years ago. Grandma Lillian always looked twenty years younger than her age. She loved the San Francisco Bay Area, never failed to make lemonade from the lemons of life, and sent a $25 check and a card for every grandchild's birthday. Since I stopped traveling on Shabbat, when she got very sick, I made arrangements on Friday to spend Shabbat in the hospital in her room at her side, an intimacy afforded me by the stringencies of Jewish law then, as today. Ten years earlier, on Shabbat afternoon, after one of many visits to my grandma's side, my mother, sister and I, and my great uncle Ed and aunt Molly, walked away from her door towards the waiting room for a few minutes of relief.

But as we headed past the nurse's station, a voice called out: "she is fading—you should come quickly." We hustled back to the room. I knelt down, took out my *siddur,* and began to recite the *vidui* and concluded with the *Sh'ma* prayer, the Jewish declaration of faith in God—"Hear O

Israel, the Lord our God, the Lord is one." Before I finished the words, she had died.

So it is with dread and duty that I kneel at Joel's bed, and hold his hands, and open the rabbi's manual to chant the words of that prayer again. It is with love for Joel and God and fear of death and losing him that I conclude with the *Sh'ma* and look up. And it is with a sense of relief, relief that he is still fighting, relief that if he does die, the rite has been done. It is with a sense of relief that I finish the *Sh'ma*, look up, and nothing happens. It is not a spell; it is a prayer. It is only God who gives life and takes it away, a thought that gives me only a little comfort in this moment.

11

Exile and Loss

Elie Wiesel once wrote about his life in the period soon after the *Shoah*: "I felt like a stranger. I had lost my faith, and thus, my sense of belonging and orientation. My faith in life was covered in ashes; my faith in humanity was laughable; my faith in God was shaken." I feel at home in the writings of Elie Wiesel.

Joel was a rabbinical student. He was *my* student in *my* class on Jewish prayer. If I felt that Joel's devotion to Judaism should *count for something*, whatever that may mean, it is only because the calculus—that devotion to God will bring a reward—is what we are taught. It is a calculus with devastating consequences to faith in the very same God to Whom it seeks to inspire devotion.

The Torah rarely promises a specific reward for any of its commandments, but in two peculiar instances, we are promised one—long life—for honoring one's parents (Exodus 20:12, Deuteronomy 5:16), and the corollary of that commandment for animals, sending away a mother bird when taking its eggs or chicks (Deuteronomy 22:6–7). Long life may not be promised if you observe other commandments, but these two *mitzvot* seem to hold the key to a long(er) life.

All of this is background to understand the story the rabbis tell, whether imagined or remembered, about one of their own named Elisha Ben Abuya. He is the rabbi who, one day, gives up on God, and simply walks away. Why? Elisha Ben Abuya, known simply as *acher*, the "other," after his apostasy, once sees a boy on a ladder who is instructed by his father to send away the mother bird so they can take the young. The boy climbs a ladder at the behest of his father, and in the midst of fulfilling two commandments, both of which explicitly promise long life, the boy falls off the ladder and dies. Abuya declares, "There is judgment, and there is no Judge."

Did Elisha know the boy? Or was it enough for him to see a child, any child, lying dead on the ground, for him to say, "I give up. I can't take You anymore," to walk away and wander the earth, like Cain, in exile from God?

12

Saturday, November 18, 2007

The sky turns from the dark black of night to the navy blue of morning because somewhere the sun is preparing to rise and bring a new day. It is eight o'clock. I sit next to Heather. She sits near Joel's head and shoulders and caresses his chest as it rises and falls to the beat of a ventilator.

"He's holding on," I say. "Maybe he's enjoying the rhythm of the pumps and drips and beeps, improvising a jazz song." Even now, I imagine, Joel is finding music in the world. Heather smiles faintly for a moment and goes back to stroking his hair.

I look across the room and see the bottle of kosher grape juice Reb Mimi gave me. Before the boys went home last night, we made *Kiddush* and, in doing so, fulfilled the commandment to remember Shabbat, the seventh day on which God rested from all of the work which He had done, having declared the world and all He had made "very good." This morning, I turn to Heather and say to her, "we should make the *Kiddush* for the Sabbath day."

She looks at me like I am crazy. Truth be told, after the words leave my mouth, I think maybe I am too. "Why?" she asks, and in my mind, I feel the force of her question. Why make *Kiddush* now? Why celebrate anything here? Grape juice is a substitute for wine and wine is a symbol of joy (Proverbs teaches, "Wine gladdens the heart") and what the hell kind of joy do I feel? And God? Let's not even go there.

"Joel loves *Kiddush*," I say gently. "He loves the grape juice and the prayers, and he is still in this world, and it is Shabbat in this world, Shabbat morning, and he should hear *Kiddush* and rejoice for Shabbat." That's the secret of being real: everything with tears and joy. I pour a cup and sing, "*V'shamru bnei Yisrael et haShabbat l'dorotam brit olam...*"—"The children of Israel will keep the Shabbat for the generations, an everlasting promise between Me and the children of Israel, an everlasting sign. For in six days God made the heavens and the earth and on the seventh day, God rested and was refreshed." I don't think I ever said *Kiddush*, such a blessing of joy, amidst such total despair. I think it is the only *Kiddush* I will ever really say. The nurses' shift changes. The nurses who arrive tell us on their first visit, "it is not looking good," trying to warn us the moment is not far away.

13

Friends

It is an understatement to say that what is happening should not be happening. Heather and Joel and the boys should be with Joel's classmates, spending the third year of rabbinical school in Jerusalem, studying Torah and falling in love with Israel, its land, its people. They should be eating hummus and falafel and admiring the olives and fish at the *shuk*, the open-air market. They should be with Deborah and Noam, two of Joel's rabbinical school classmates who both love him like a brother. Heather has Deborah's phone number in Israel in her cell phone. We call. It starts to ring and Heather hands me the phone, turns away and weeps.

"Deborah, it's Daniel. I'm here with Joel."

"Daniel, we've been so worried. What's happening?"

"Deborah, it's very serious. He doesn't have long."

"How long do they think?"

"Minutes, maybe hours."

Deborah audibly gasps. "Oh my God. No. That close? No..."

Heather looks back at me. "Heather wants to talk to you," I tell Deborah. "Let me put her on the phone."

I do not hear what is said. They are words spoken with eyes closed, and love.

"I'm going to put the phone up to Joel's ear," Heather says to Deborah, "so you can talk to him." She stands and holds it near Joel's ear for a few moments. They talk for another minute. Heather asks her to find Noam and tell him to call soon, and says good-bye. We place the cell phone on the bed and wait for it to ring again. While we wait, we give to Joel what we can give. Song. Prayer. Touch. Love.

Noam calls a few minutes later. It is 9:15 AM. Heather picks up the phone, hears his voice, and starts to cry. "I want you to talk to him, Noam. I'm going to put you on speaker and put the phone near his ear."

There are images and sounds that sear themselves into your memory. When I was young, the phone rang one morning. My father answered it and I heard him crying through the door of his bedroom. I was only seven or eight years old, but I still remember the sound of my father crying. I found out later his mother, my grandma Beatrice, had said to him, "Howard, Arthur won't wake up. He is very blue, and cold. I'm scared."

I remember they brought me to see my Grandpa Arthur lying in an open coffin, dressed in a suit with a shirt that looked stuffed and too tight. His face was pale white, stretched taut. I remember other images of my grandfather from pictures I have seen since, but I struggle to recall a visual image of him alive from my own memories. I remember the feel of his whiskers and the look of his cane, and a shaking quality to his voice, but what I see in my mind's eye are only images of pictures. The image seared into my memory is my grandfather lying there, in his coffin.

I will never forget how Noam's voice called out through the tiny speaker of the cell phone into Joel's ear. It is seared into my memory. "Joel! Joel!" he pleaded. "No. ..No. . .Please hold on. . .No! No. . .Joel. . ."

Heather listens and cries and takes the phone in her hands, speaks in a soft, patient, soothing voice, "Noam, it's okay Noam. Noam. . ." I turn my head and cry and cannot stop.

14

9:42 AM

Joel's pulse slows from 80 to 70 to 60 to 50 beats per minute. His blood pressure falls even further. 35 over 34? It is the red number on the screen. Heather stands on Joel's left side with her mom, Paula, holding her hand. Rabbi K, a rabbinical school friend who arrived just after dawn, sits at Joel's feet and says the *Sh'ma* softly again and again. I stand at Joel's right side. The beeps from the machines slow further. I kneel between the tubes and machines and bow my head on Joel's arm, holding it in despair and trembling. His hands, which had brought music into the world—vibrant, jumping, joyous music, life-giving music into the world—his hands are now cold. I start to cry again, to sing, and to give the angels permission to take him, to let him go.

> *Shalom aleichem, malachei hasharet, malachei elyon, mi'melech*
> *malchei hamilachim, HaKadosh Baruch Hu*
> *Boachem l'shalom, malachei hashalom, malachei elyon, mi'melech*
> *malchei hamilachim, HaKadosh Baruch Hu*
> *Barchuni l'shalom, malachei hashalom, malachei elyon, mi'melech*
> *malchei hamilachim, HaKadosh Baruch Hu*
> *Tze'tchem l'shalom, malachei hashalom, malachei elyon, mi'melech*
> *malchei hamilachim, HaKadosh Baruch Hu*

> Peace be unto you, ye ministering angels, angels of the Most High, the supreme King of Kings, the Holy Blessing One.
> Come in peace, ye angels of peace, angels of the Most High, the supreme King of Kings, the Holy Blessing One.
> Bless me with peace, ye angels of peace, ye angels of the Most High, the supreme King of Kings, the Holy Blessing One.
> Leave in peace, ye angels of peace, angels of the Most High, the supreme King of Kings, the Holy Blessing One.

The melody fades away. I open my eyes. There are more poetic ways to say it: that he left this world; he passed on; he slipped away; his soul fled. But death is stark and blue, permanent and cold. Joel is dead.

15

November 17, 2007. After

What remains is movement of the respirator pushing Joel's chest up and down.

Numbers and lines come to a rest on monitors. We hold one another and cry and cry. The doctor must be called to declare the official time of death. 9:42 AM, Saturday, November 17th, 2007. We ask for nothing to be done. Give us quiet.

The nurses turn off the monitors and the tubes. They file out to the hallway. A great effort has come to an end.

I step outside. Can a social worker come to help us think about how to tell the boys? The nurses come in to remove the tubes and clean the body. This they do with Heather, who cares for her husband beyond the end.

She comes to see me in the hall. "Daniel, they want to put him in a bag and zip it up. Is that okay?"

"Yes, it's okay. If you'd rather it not be zipped up all the way, it can be unzipped at the top, but his face should be covered with a cloth somehow."

The rationale for this practice, of covering the body, has its basis in a Talmudic concept known as *kvod hamet*, honoring the dead. One manifestation of this idea is that the body is never left unattended between the time of death and burial. To escort and bury the dead is a *hesed shel emet*—a true act of loving kindness—for it can never be repaid. Another way we honor the dead is by covering the body, because the rabbis understood it to be inappropriate to look upon a dead person: "Those who cannot look at us should not be looked upon."

In the room, it is quieter now that the ventilator is off. The whir of a small pump can be heard, necessary because a body left without muscle tone will ooze. Paula and I join Heather to sit with Joel. Tears stream down Heather's face and stop again. Her eyes are red and tired. She turns to me and says, "I don't understand. Am I just supposed to go home now?"

Within her question are a thousand more. How do I begin again? How do I return to a home without him? What do I say to my children? I have cried so much, fought so many hours—does it all end so suddenly?

I don't know what else to say except, "Yes. The battle is over. This part of the journey is done."

But it is not time to go home. An hour before, Heather called Sue, the nanny, and told her to bring the kids to the hospital. They will be here soon. Paula volunteers to stay with Joel's body while I take Heather to get something to eat. She has eaten little in days and will need her strength for the afternoon.

We walk quietly towards The Bistro when I turn to her. "Do you know how you are going to tell them?" I want to help her be a little prepared for a moment one should never, and can never, ever be ready for. How do you look in your children's eyes and expel the sound that will break their hearts without crying and sobbing endlessly yourself?

"I think I do," she says. "Daddy was trying really hard to fight off the cancer but he couldn't. His body was too weak and there were lots of infections and this morning, Daddy died. It wasn't anyone's fault. It wasn't Daddy's fault, or your fault, or Mommy's fault, or the doctors' fault. Daddy's body just couldn't fight anymore."

I look at her in awe. I will never know from where she found strength to go on. "I just want a tuna on wheat. I can't be here anymore. I have to go back upstairs," she says and walks away.

Joel's mother died when he was young. His father, too, is gone. Joel yearned, ached, to see what his mother did not, to see his sons grow up. Many years from now, his sons will want, more than anything, to see their own sons grow old because their father died when they were young.

I return to Joel's body so that, when the boys arrive, Heather and Paula can meet them at the hospital entrance. The nanny takes Ellis for a walk. I am not in the small meditation room outside the ICU where Coleman and Miles were told. I come in only a few minutes later. Coleman has thin blond hair; he is curled up in his grandmother's arms and tears stream out of his big eyes, down his soft cheeks, while Miles pushes and scratches and pinches his mom. He is smaller than his big brother, is a brilliant child and has a talent for acting. He will not cry. It seems to me he wants to burst out of the room and run away but, being in a small room, he will only lash out. Heather is more than patient. "You can't hurt Mommy. You're having a big feeling. You're sad, and it's okay to cry. But you can't hurt Mommy."

Heather and the boys visit Joel. Coleman hugs his father's sheet-covered torso a final time. Miles asks concrete questions: "Is Daddy under there?" "Is Daddy's head up here?" "Can we go home soon?" I take the older boys to the bathroom. Heather spends a final few moments with Ellis and Joel's body while we load the minivan. I come back upstairs to stay with Joel, and then, just like that, Heather and the boys leave.

I stay the rest of the afternoon with Joel's body along with Avi, a close friend of Joel's who had stayed with and helped the boys get to the hospital this morning. We pray *mincha*, the afternoon service, together. As we chant the opening prayer, Psalm 145, I hear Avi laugh bitterly as we read: "Adonai guards all those who love Him." I like Avi's laughter, agree with it; it seems a more cutting cry against God to use words from a psalm.

We eat a small *seudat shlishit*, the third Shabbat meal. Shabbat afternoon is a time of both perfection and great sadness. It is a time we dream of a perfect world, of God's oneness, of a time when this world's veil of brokenness and pain will be lifted and a new world will come. Yet, as the sun sinks in the sky, it is a time of sadness, for the world remains unredeemed. There are sad, yearning, mournful songs sung each Shabbat afternoon; Avi and I start to sing them with Joel, or *for* Joel, at the foot of his bed waiting for a new week to begin. Melody and song usually connect me to prayer, to God; it was something Joel and I shared. But Joel, a lover of God, lies dead before me, and song now feels like an abomination. I let my voice trail off and let Avi continue alone. I have no more songs to sing.

The bottle of grape juice Reb Mimi gave me nearly 30 hours ago is two-thirds empty from *Kiddush* Friday night and Shabbat morning. Evening begins; Avi empties the bottle and chants *havdalah*, a prayer to mark the end of Shabbat, the beginning of a new week, the distinction between what is holy and profane, between light and darkness. We drink. I bid Joel goodbye. Avi will wait with him until the *chevra kaddisha*, the holy Jewish burial society, arrives a few hours later.

Fifteen years before, when Jay and I roomed together, it was a cold, rainy afternoon in February when I returned to our apartment at Maple and Noyes after swim practice. I put down my bags, and heard Jay playing our rented, upright piano with a tinny sound that echoed on the neighbor's ceiling below us. He was playing Billy Joel—I don't remember what song it was anymore but it was full of blues and melancholy. His eyes were closed and he was singing loudly to the air above the piano. I crossed the threshold into the living room and Jay opened his eyes, stopped, and let the pedal echo on the last chord he hit. "The big bad wolf is back," Jay said, and started playing again. That was what Jay called the leukemia he battled as a child, the leukemia that would kill him a few years later.

The ground floor lobby at City of Hope is lit by dim fluorescents. I step out of the elevator and see the same man at the visitor's desk who was there Friday morning when I arrived, the same man who called Joel by his first name, who knew Heather had gone to breakfast. I walk towards the front door but, before I leave, I turn around and call to him. "The big bad wolf was stronger."

"I'm so sorry," is all he can say.

Another friend of mine is dead.

chapter 4

The Journey to the Funeral

Thick was the darkness
And there was no light.
He could see neither
What was ahead nor behind.
For days he traveled in this blindness
Without a light to guide him,
Ascending or descending,
He could not be sure,
Going on with only
The companionship of grief
In which he felt [his dead friend] Enkidu at his side.

—THE EPIC OF GILGAMESH

1

The Funeral Journey

I arrive home, hug Jen, re-live the story by telling it, and collapse from exhaustion and despair. Sunday morning, I tell our boys and hold them as they cry, confused that their *abba* and *imma* are crying, confused that their friends' *abba*, that their friend Joel, is dead. I try to reassure them that I will not die just because their friends' *abba* did. In between these wrenching conversations, I spend Sunday making arrangements for Jen and me to get to Dallas for the funeral, scheduled for Monday, and for the boys to be taken care of while we are gone. Joel's body flies on an American Airlines flight Sunday afternoon.

We arrive Sunday night around 1:00 AM, rent a car, and arrive at the hotel at 2:30 AM. I cannot sleep. While I have been to funerals before, this time I wonder about the journey *to* a funeral. The journey from death leads back to the ground ("dust to dust"), to a place beyond, to heaven, or God. But to where does the journey to a funeral lead? It is a journey to a journey; a pilgrimage to escort those I love, or their bodies, to the border of this world.

Jewish tradition teaches that going to a funeral is so holy it supersedes all other *mitzvot*, even the study of Torah. If we encounter a dead body with nobody to bury it, we must abandon all other tasks to accompany the dead to their resting place. But where does the pilgrimage of accompanying the dead lead? To sorrow? To honesty? There is an awareness which can only be achieved through grief and death. It is a journey beneath the surface of our lives, a reminder of that which bubbles beneath. It is a pause between the notes, a silence that only gazing at the grave provides.

I think too about the funeral itself. I am the director of a summer camp, not the rabbi of a synagogue. I am relieved not to be conducting Joel's funeral, but I wonder, if I were, what would I say about God and why this happened? I think about the words of the psalmist: "God guards those who love Him," and how I liked Avi's laughter against God. I wonder how a rabbi can scoff at a psalm. If some of my campers were here, what would I say to them? That it seems like a sick joke to say, "God guards those who love Him"?

If I worked in advertising, it'd be different. At work, you just sell the brand—United Airlines, Nabisco. So what if I use the product or care about it. My Judaism, my questions and doubts—they would be my own business. But when you're a rabbi, your life, your faith are themselves teaching material. People look at you, they look to you, to see how a person of faith responds. The Talmud taught, "One's inside should be like one's outside." If you're a rabbi who doesn't actually believe what you're teaching, well, I'd rather work in advertising than be fake.

Rabbis are supposed to know what they believe. People ask "where is God?" and "why did these things happen?" and rabbis are supposed to have answers. I wonder what this means about the path I've chosen. I wonder if I shouldn't just be a lawyer or go into business. Or maybe I should become a swim coach, and help people be healthy—that would be a fitting tribute to my dead friends. But how can I be a rabbi if I laugh angrily at God in a moment of crisis? How can I provide consolation when I myself need comfort?

I think about Jay's funeral so many years ago, and the rabbi who offered me a symbolic spade, and I wonder if I'd be able to do much better. Back then, I didn't even know the questions to ask; now I have many more, but no answers, at least not ones a rabbi should give. Is being a rabbi the right path for me after all? It is 4:30 AM when sleep finally takes me.

The funeral is in the large sanctuary of Congregation Shearith Israel, where Joel and Heather were long-time members. I have known Joel only a few years, and as the senior rabbi, Bill Gershon, speaks, I realize I know only glimpses of Joel's greatness, that many rabbis before have called him student and friend:

> I met Joel on my first High Holidays in 1998. I stood in front of the congregation and there was this young guy conducting the choir. He had this glow and a smile on his face. It wasn't long after that Joel and I began to meet regularly. I remember Passover Seders and other holiday meals spent together.
>
> Joel, you were my *talmid muvhaq*—the most important student a rabbi can have. You meant so much to me, and to Raquel and our family. You brought such joy into our lives.
>
> When Joel told me he was applying to rabbinical school, I was thrilled. When he was accepted to both the Jewish Theological Seminary in New York and the Ziegler School of Rabbinic Studies in Los Angeles, I was so proud. I knew the Jewish people would never be the same.

Rabbi Adam Raskin is the assistant rabbi at Shearith Israel. He speaks about Joel's love of children, and their love of him:

> Every week, in the Shabbat morning children's service that Joel led, he always featured the same story, with the same dramatic moment. Each week Joel would retell the story of Bil'am, the pagan prophet who was determined to curse the Jewish people. With all his charisma, Joel would build up that moment when Bil'am blessed instead of cursed the Jewish people.
>
> My daughter Nessa, then only a toddler, would be on the edge of her *tuches* every week upon hearing that story, and she would scrunch up her face as if Joel was going to make some visible curse appear right there before her eyes.

But, of course, the story would always end the same way…as Bil'am blurted out *mah tovu ohalecha Ya'akov*, "how beautiful are your dwelling places, O Jacob. . ." Nessa and every other kid would breathe a sigh of relief. . .Thank God, another week, another curse averted! And the place would break out in song.

Joel brought that joy to our kids every Shabbat—and to their parents as well; and how they loved to help Mr. Joel read the Torah; or help Mr. Joel lead the parade; or help Mr. Joel say the *brachot* (the blessings); or answer one of Mr. Joel's questions; or sit right up in front of Mr. Joel as he would teach them some beautiful gem, some life lesson packaged in an understandable, digestible child-sized nugget from that week's Torah portion.

He would do anything to excite a child's imagination about Torah. How many of us remember the Purim when all the talk around the *shul* was "Have you seen Mr. Joel?" He shaved his trademark beard that year, and revealed that gentle boyish face that reminds me of Heather and Joel's wedding picture in the photo montage on his online Care Page. The kids were fascinated to see Joel's clean-shaven face. Some just stared; others wanted to touch it. He was a marvel, he was a magnet.

Prayers are said, the service concludes. Joel is buried in an old Jewish cemetery that has history and character. His parents are buried here. "Joel will like this," I think to myself. We follow the procession back to the *shiva* home, and Jennifer and I help Heather and the boys settle in while the community begins to arrive. We eat and drink and say our good-byes for now; we leave to catch a late afternoon flight.

2

Displaced

Back in LA, we unpack and immediately re-pack our bags. Jen's mom is turning 60 and, Tuesday night, quite bizarrely, we land in Atlanta for a long weekend—Thanksgiving dinner and a birthday party with family and friends. I am in a stupor; there and not there at all, both at the same time.

Before Thanksgiving dinner, I walk in a botanical garden, and, in the stunning yellow and orange and red colors of autumn, it strikes me that the leaves are discolored because they have been cut off from their source of life. I can think only of Joel's body, jaundiced and blue in his last hours. During Thanksgiving dinner, I eat quietly. On Friday, our family drives to a science museum downtown. As we pull out of the underground parking lot, I scrape the side of our rented minivan against a large concrete pole. I am elsewhere, in a daze, displaced.

Joel would want me to be here, with my family, to carry on with life. On the other hand, I clearly should not be in Atlanta. I am in mourning. That Joel was my friend, not a blood brother, is a distinction without a difference. It is said, "You pick your friends; relatives are thrust upon you." Why should I mourn less for a soul I picked in fellowship?

Jewish law makes no demands upon friends, even best friends, to say the *kaddish*, to sit *shiva*. I wish it wasn't up to me. I long to be commanded by the tradition in which I found such meaning in Israel many years ago; I long to be included within the circle of the Law, but I feel cast out by that which should embrace me. I should be sitting *shiva* with Heather and the boys, not on a long weekend for a festive dinner.

Shiva would have meant I never left the home of mourning in Dallas. Jewish law would have obligated me to set Thanksgiving and a birthday celebration aside, to acknowledge in fullness my loss. It would have meant stopping life, not shaving or showering, not leaving home for a week. It would have meant covering the mirrors and sitting on the ground, and saying *kaddish*. Jewish tradition obligates children mourning their parents to say *kaddish* three times daily for eleven months. Mothers and fathers, sisters and brothers and spouses are only obligated for thirty days, although nowadays many people mourn longer, especially to say *kaddish*.

It is an irony of Jewish history that the mourner's *kaddish* developed from the longer "rabbi's *kaddish*," which was said by a teacher and his students when they finished learning and left one another's company. When a teacher died, his students said the *kaddish* to mourn that their learning had ended for the final time. From that graveside farewell prayer, the mourner's *kaddish* was born. But instead of including everyone with a close relationship with someone who died, the obligation devolved only upon the seven relatives. History closed the mourner's circle—and left friends out of the law's obligation. I yearn to be obligated, but as a friend, Jewish law cruelly sets me free. I feel betrayed, exiled.

Elizabeth DeVita Raeburn, the sister of "the boy in the bubble" (a young boy who suffered from a compromised immune system and spent most of his life isolated from human contact), wrote a book about sibling loss called *The Empty Room*. In it, she describes how, when people suffer unrecognized loss, "there are no rituals to mark them—no wakes, funerals, sympathy cards, or meals made by neighbors; no social recognition whatsoever that a loss has occurred." Harder still, I think, is to watch the rituals unfold, even to participate in them by helping the "real mourners" say *kaddish* and sit *shiva*, but to be told by the tradition that those rituals are not really for you.

"Validation," writes DeVita-Raeburn, "is what moves you out of the frozen place after a loss." I wonder if I haven't been frozen all these years after I left Jay's home and flew across country alone; if I need to fully mourn not only Joel's death, but Jay's too.

Mourning for a friend poses another question: how do you mourn for the friend you would have turned to for help? Jay and Joel—I miss them both. But it's not just that. I need them too.

On Saturday night at the party, I take a long walk in the cool autumn night, more comfortable in solitude than company. Joel's death reawakens in me questions that lay dormant since Jay's death nearly eleven years before; it forces me to question my answers and wonder whether the path I chose is true. I can no longer return to the young man I once was. If I try and ignore God, I will only be pretending God is not there. The possibility of the hidden-ness of God's hidden-ness is gone for me. If I walk away, I cannot return to the innocence of my childhood and adolescence, when I simply did not know that being in relationship with God was an option. I will leave God with Joel's body, dead in room 3209. I will do so in anger and rage at His injustice.

Joel loved You, God. What did you do with his love? You killed him. Why do You take my friends? Why should I care about You, pray to You, when, at best, You are absent, or worse, so cruel?

3

November 28, 2007

In the *Shoah*, the Holocaust, many Jewish parents faced a devastating choice: stay together and die as a family, or give your children to the Christian community, hiding their identity so they might live. After the war ended, some parents survived and went in search of the children they'd given up years before. To find Jewish children in displaced person camps filled with orphaned children, it is said that aid workers were instructed to sing loudly, "*Sh'ma Yisrael*," and if a child turned his or her head, they knew the child was Jewish. Years before, Jewish mothers and fathers had sung that child to sleep with the words of the *Sh'ma*. Still the children remembered.

It is Wednesday, nine days since we laid Joel to rest. Eleven days since I held his hand as he died, slipping away from me. Our middle son, Benjamin, crawls under the covers. Every night of his life, my wife and I have sung him to sleep with the words of the *Sh'ma*. It is a *mitzvah* from the Torah to say the words of the *Sh'ma* each night—"when you lie down" (Deuteronomy 6:7). Saying the *Sh'ma* reminds our children every night that they are Jews. Just as important, as parents it is our way of telling them, "You are loved. Don't be scared of the dark. We are here. God is here. Everything is going to be okay."

Sometimes I make a game out of it—I cover his eyes and he tries to wriggle away, or he hides beneath the covers and I wait for him to come out. He likes to delay the inevitable, but after a minute or two, he finally lies still. Most nights, I sing and he listens. Tonight, I ask him to sing to me. I can't get the words out of my mouth. He begins to sing. I am listening, looking away as tears roll down my face. He sees me crying and lies very still while he finishes the prayer. "Don't worry, buddy," I say, "*Abba* is just very sad that Joel died, but I'll be alright."

"Okay, *Abba*," he says. "Feel better." And as I lean down and give him a kiss, some of my tears wet his cheek.

The next morning, I am driving to work. I have not yet said the morning prayers—I plan to when I arrive to work—but the time for saying the *Sh'ma*—there is a specific time prescribed by the Torah—is slipping away. Tears well up. What has been so meaningful for me so many mornings of my life, I cannot do this morning. When one says the *Sh'ma*, one accepts the Kingdom of Heaven. It is an act of letting go, of reminding oneself that not all is in our control, that our lives are a gift from God. That is supposed to bring comfort, perspective. This morning, I do not want to accept the Kingdom of Heaven. Many things are slipping away.

The rabbis tell a story about the relationship between saying the *Sh'ma* and accepting the Kingdom of Heaven:

> Rabbi Jeremiah was once sitting before Rabbi Hiyya the son of Abba, and the latter saw that he was prolonging the word "one" very much. He said to him: Once you have declared God King over all that is above and below and over the four quarters of the heaven, no more is required" (Talmud Berachot 13b).

No more is required. Is that it? That's all? Just accept that God is King over all? The rabbis dictate that we should say a blessing both over what is good and what is evil—lest we think that God is responsible only for what is good. So: when someone dies, we say a blessing, *Baruch Dayan HaEmet*—"Blessed is the True Judge." We bless God when someone dies. It is not a blessing of thanks, but a blessing of acknowledgement that all is from God. The blessing forces us to admit that when someone leaves behind a wife bereft, and children who must grow up fatherless, that this too is from God.

Rabbis who officiate at funerals approach the seven relatives and pin a black ribbon on them. I hate the ribbon like I hated the spade the rabbi gave me years before. The ribbon is a symbolic substitution; you're supposed to tear your clothes when someone dies, not don a little ribbon. The rabbi begins the cut with scissors or a knife and, while the relatives tear, helps them bless God: "Blessed are You Lord Our God, King of the Universe, who is the Judge of Truth." I feel sick thinking about this blessing.

The point of the *Sh'ma* and the blessing when someone dies is to acknowledge that, since God is One and His judgment is true, one day in the future, the brokenness and the pain, the anguish and the tears will all be made right. God is all-good and all-knowing and all-powerful, so what we experience as bad, it's not really bad; it's just that we are small and cannot know the whole story. God is One—says the *Sh'ma*—but we cannot understand God's ways. That is what God said to Job:

> Then the Lord answered Job from the stormy wind, and said, "Who is this that darkens counsel by words without knowledge? Gird up now your loins like a man; for I will demand of you, and you will answer me. Where were you when I laid the foundations of the earth? Declare, if you have understanding. Who determined its measures, do you know? Or who has stretched the line upon it? Upon what are its foundations fastened? Or who laid its corner stone, when the morning stars sang together, and all the sons of God shouted for joy?" (Job 39:1–7)

I declare! I was not there when God laid the foundations of the earth. I do not know who determined its measures, or who stretched the line upon the world, or upon what its foundations are fastened anymore. I was not there when the morning stars sang together. I do not hear them singing today. I cannot join the sons of God who shouted for joy. In my car on the way to work, I do not understand. I have only the tears in my eyes and an obligation to accept the Kingdom of Heaven, to say the *Sh'ma* and declare God is One.

The rabbis insisted that you have to get the words out of your mouth. It is not enough to just think it; you have to *say* it, because they knew you can think things and, sometimes, it doesn't really mean anything. But God created with words, and when you put something out into the world, it has power, creative power. So they said you have to speak it into the world, that "Adonai is our God," that "God is One." Ideally, they said you should say it loud enough for your own ears to hear it, but, if you say it in a whisper, aloud but so softly you can't hear the very words from your own mouth, you have still fulfilled your obligation. You just have to get the words out. Driving in my car this morning, I do not want to get the words out. Nor is my son, Benjamin, here to sing them to me.

I used to wonder, who says the *Sh'ma* so softly that he can't hear the very words come from his own mouth? Who? I wondered. Someone sick, of course. Someone for whom it is hard to speak, hard to breathe, in fact. Maybe someone taking his last breath. Or someone who just can't stomach the idea of what he's saying.

I think I understand what is happening to me—I see myself in deep sadness but, for all the wisdom, I cannot stop the feelings. I cannot stop the pain, though I put on a face for the world, drive to work and drink coffee. I am in mourning. Like a blood relative, I should say *kaddish*, desist from attending big parties, stop walking through the world as if nothing has changed and everything is the same.

If I had to counsel someone else, I would tell them, "go to daily *minyan*. Take on an obligation to say *kaddish* for your friend, perhaps only for a week or two instead of thirty days. That way, you acknowledge the loss but preserve a difference between what one does for relatives and what one does for a friend." Jewish law does not actually *forbid* a friend from saying *kaddish* or taking on some other mourning customs—Rabbi Moses Isserles, an important Jewish legal authority, wrote, "Should a person be stringent upon himself and mourn someone he is not obligated to mourn.

. .there is no reason to deter him from doing so" (Shulchan Aruch, Yoreh De'ah, 374:6)—but fulfilling the traditions because you choose to feels less meaningful because it is like you are doing something that is a creation of your own desire, rather than a response to something (Someone?) larger than yourself. "Greater is the one who is commanded and does," teaches the Talmud, "than one who is not commanded and does." As strange as that teaching sounds, making your own religion misses the point; it just sends you back to yourself, when what you need is to be part of something more.

Nevertheless, because I *understand* I am in mourning—emotionally—even though Jewish law tells me otherwise, I also try to suspend ultimate judgment against God for a while, until the pain is not so raw. "Do not try to appease a man in his anger," say the rabbis. So I try not to appease myself. I try to continue to observe the practices that have sustained me for so long, to let myself rebel against God through what He asks of me, to rebel against prayer through prayer.

Finally I say it. I get the words out. I do not refuse because. . .why? Because, despite how distant I feel from God, how angry and confused and sad I feel—I did not exercise; I am eating too much, things I recognize that go with depression—I want to find God through the words. When I found Him long ago in Israel, the experience beneath the desert sky did not endure. What lasted, what has sustained me, was the discipline of regular prayer and study, of showing up and moving forward even when I didn't feel like it or understand.

Saying the words of the prayer is not an expression to God of how I feel. It is an attempt at connection. "Where is God found in this world?" asks Rabbi Menachem Mendel of Kotzk. "Wherever we let Him in." So I try to say the words, to let God in.

I think of Joel. He, too, is why I say the *Sh'ma*. Even as he sat in his own hospital bed, dying from a cancer that ruined his body but did not wreck his soul, he comforted me. He prayed. He loved God. He loved the tradition and saying the *Sh'ma*. If he could say it, how can I not? If his experience did not wreck his soul, how can I let it wreck mine? So Joel helps me pray, to speak God's Oneness into the world, even though I don't see Oneness. I don't see unity. I don't see how it all makes sense. I feel tears behind my eyes. I see children without a father who himself grew up a child without a father. In solidarity with fatherless children, I do not want to accept and love my Father in Heaven, who took away a great, sweet, patient loving father.

I have sensed God's Oneness before. I have felt joy deeper than the sea and higher than the mountains when my own sons were born. So many times, the words of the *Sh'ma* helped my children fall to sleep, to believe in safety and goodness in the world. I believed them once before. And because I remember, because I can see myself mourning in my car, and because Joel was ravaged by cancer but saw through the darkness to the Oneness—even though so many things are slipping away, including the time to say the *Sh'ma* this morning—the words finally do leave my mouth. I pray in soft, exhaled breaths that are almost pants, that remind me of what Joel's last breath might have sounded like had there not been a ventilator. I say the *Sh'ma*, and the sounds do not even reach my ears, which is a relief, for I cannot bear to hear what they mean. "Hear O Israel: Adonai, our God, Adonai is One."

4

Hanukkah

Hanukkah means "dedication"—the holiday commemorates the re-dedication of the Temple. According to rabbinic lore, when the Temple was retaken, a jar of oil was found, enough for one day. It was lit, but, miraculously, it burned for eight days, the eight days of the miracle, the eight days of Hanukkah.

Our kids love fire. A few years ago, I bought a special *menorah* with small glass containers for oil, not wax candles. We placed a table near the window so the flames would be visible to people walking by, fulfilling the *mitzvah* of *pirsuma d'nisa*—publicizing the miracle. Each night, we filled the cups with olive oil and carefully placed wicks halfway in the oil and halfway outside. I told them the story of when I lit candles in the desert in Israel and how they struggled to stay lit against the wind. I told them it's never been easy, but God has always helped the Jewish people to survive. We lit the candles, turned out the lights and quietly watched the flames. Then we ate *latkes* (potato pancakes cooked in oil) and spun *dreidels* (special Hanukkah tops) for chocolate *gelt* (small coins) late into the night.

Tonight, the holiday feels dry to me, drained of its joy. We say the blessings and light candles in the living room. It doesn't mean so much to me. It seems dead, fake, like a performance we're doing for the kids. I don't have the energy to try and make it something more. So we feed them some *gelt*, announce bedtime and put them to sleep.

The house is quiet. I change into my pajamas and climb into bed early. On my night table is a book called, *Be Still and Get Going*, by Rabbi Alan Lew. I decide to read for a while before going to sleep. Maybe I'll find some inspiration from him, so I open up to a passage about Hanukkah. Rabbi Lew points to a problem: if you think about the oil story, there's only seven days of miracles, not eight. The first day, the ration of oil burned just like you'd expect; no miracle there; it's the other seven days that were miraculous. But the holiday is eight days. Strange. Rabbi Lew says this conundrum was with us for centuries and addressed in many ways but none in a compelling, satisfying way. Until Professor Shaul Lieberman of the Jewish Theological Seminary discovered an older Talmudic manuscript.

The accepted language of the story of the oil was "…this jar did not have enough oil in it except for one day's burning." "Except" from the Hebrew word *eleh* which was abbreviated as *aleph*—the first letter of the Hebrew alphabet. In the manuscript Lieberman found, the aleph was spelled out and it wasn't *eleh* at all; it was *afilu*, which means "even." So actually the story was "…this jar did not have enough oil in it for *even* one day's burning." In other words, there wasn't enough oil for a single, full day—so the miracle was the seven days and the first day too…together, eight days, problem solved.

But Rabbi Lew lingers over the implications—by this change, the meaning is entirely changed. He writes, "Before, the miracle was that the light burned against great odds, longer than we could have had any reason to expect it to burn. Now the miracle is that the light flared up at all… this is not the miracle of overcoming impossible odds, this is the miracle of the world arising out of emptiness, out of nothing."

I put the book down, turn out the lights. As I lie awake in the darkness, I think about Joel and his all-too-short life. I wonder if the miracle of our lives is not that we endure like the oil on the last seven days, but that we are called out of nothingness, that we exist at all. But life does not feel like a miracle. It feels cruel, sad.

5

Phoenix, AZ

It is the third week of December and I am on a business trip in Phoenix. My flight lands in the afternoon. I rent a car, drive to one of the local synagogues, meet with the rabbi and religious school principal for a while to talk about Ramah, and then the time for my presentation comes. All of the classes gather restlessly in the sanctuary where a TV and DVD player have been wheeled in on a cart and placed awkwardly in front of the large cantor's table. Parents walk in at the back and talk to one another—we purposefully do the presentation at the end of Hebrew school so that parents who are picking up their children will see it.

I have done this presentation hundreds of times. I greet the kids, turn on the DVD, hand out some toys for children who can tell me what activities they saw in the video, and finish by handing out brochures and applications and telling the kids they did a great job. I linger for a few minutes longer answering questions. I reassure anxious Jewish parents not to worry about sending their children away for a month. When everyone's gone, I get into the rental car and drive to a hotel. It is Tuesday night. I have a presentation tomorrow at another synagogue.

In the morning, I put on my *tallit* and *tefillin* in the hotel room and try to pray. Nothing happens. I don't feel connected to the Jewish people. I have an inbox full of emails. It feels like a waste of time. I don't care which way is east towards Jerusalem. I wonder what I'm doing, putting black boxes onto my head and arm, like they're some sort of amulet or lucky charm. I run through the words of the prayers as quickly as I can, take off the prayer garb, and put on shorts, an old t-shirt and my running shoes.

The treadmill is broken in the hotel gym. I turn around and leave, walk through the lobby and the parking lot and start to run on quiet paths next to a busy street with my water bottle in hand. I am out of shape. I haven't exercised in weeks. I run for a while, then walk, then run again. My breathing quickens. As it does, I notice the movement of my chest; it goes up and down, up and down. I think of Joel's broad chest spread wide by a ventilator; it continued to rise and fall until the doctor came to declare his time of death. I stop running and stand in place. My chest continues to rise and fall.

I look down an empty street filled with tan and pink houses; they all look the same. I am a long ways from "the point" in Arad and the mountains of Jordan. I think of my childhood spent working out in the pool, shooting hoops on Jay's driveway, being strong and in shape. I think about how I am decaying, that we are all decaying, and I wonder how I came to this: out of breath after not yet a mile. I think of my sadness, and how there is no answer to life and its decay, and I think of my children, so young. A wave of anguish rushes over me: "What have I done? To bring them into this world." I turn around and return slowly back to the hotel.

6

Wednesday, January 9, 2008

Shiva is past. *Shloshim*—the first 30 days after someone dies—is over, too. During the 23 days between *shiva* and *shloshim*, many restrictions are lifted—one can leave the house, sit on chairs and wear leather shoes, one can study Torah, resume marital relations, and return to work. But many restrictions remain—one should not go to large concerts and celebrations, or get a haircut or shave, or go to a spa, or get married. After *shloshim*, only one who has lost a parent is technically considered a mourner.

Why is so much longer allotted to mourn a parent? For better or worse, our connection with our parents is the formative relationship in defining who we are as people. That makes sense to me. But when I think that Jewish law no longer recognizes Heather as a mourner after thirty days, it seems cruel, a ridiculously short amount of time to acknowledge her loss. I advise her differently; I recommend she continue to say *kaddish*. Her journey is not at an end; in many ways, it is only beginning. But somehow I can't give myself the same permission to acknowledge the depth of my own grief. I continue to mourn alone.

Less and less, I mark time in hours and days and weeks since Joel left this world. It is more than a month now, but I don't want to mark in months the time since he died. It feels callous. I feel guilty. Not guilt for something I did wrong, like cheating on a test. Or for something I did not do, like not calling my wife. I feel guilty for forgetting, for healing, for just being alive. I remain in the world. I am a husband and a father. Joel is not.

My family and I vacationed in late December at a rental home in Mendocino on the rugged California coast, a few hours north of San Francisco. The home had a view, and I spent many hours on the deck outside with the cold, moist winds blowing on my face; and inside, warm, watching the ocean behind picture windows.

My wife, Jennifer knows I still need some time away. Two of my friends from rabbinical school now work in Houston. One has a congregant who owns a condominium in Galveston, Texas. When they invite me to come spend time together, Jennifer encourages me to go. I arrive late Sunday morning and the three of us hang out together in Galveston until they have to return to work on Monday afternoon. I can stay. I can enjoy a condominium in Galveston, Texas, with a view of the cool, rolling waters of the Gulf of Mexico. Once my friends are gone, I am alone for two nights and three days until Wednesday afternoon.

Being here by myself is a wonderful gift and poses an interesting challenge: what will I do with this precious time? Whether we like it or not, how we spend our time reflects what we really want. Our choices reflect not who we say we want to be, but who we really are. I have a condo with a view, a health club, plenty of kosher food, TV with cable, my computer, some books, my *tallit*, *tefillin* and a *siddur*. Nobody but me will know how I decide to spend these two nights and three days of my life. Will I watch TV all day, or work out at the health club? Will I say blessings before I eat the food I have here? Or will I eat non-kosher food at one of the local restaurants? Will I pray? Time interrogates me. Here are two nights and three days. How will you use them? Is now the time your faith unravels?

I used to struggle with waking up early enough to make it to *minyan* or to pray at home. The struggle shifted from fatigue to busy-ness—life was so hectic, I had to learn to carve out time to pray between kids and work, email and errands. Now the challenge is not so much time management. It is doubt, anger.

I wake around 7:30 AM, get dressed, and walk onto the patio. I drape the *tallit* around me, wrap the arm *tefillin* around my left arm, and place the head *tefillin* on the top of my forehead. The last step is to re-wrap the *tefillin* around my third and fourth fingers and, as I do so, to say a verse from Hosea (1:21–22), "I betroth myself to You forever; I betroth myself to You with justice and judgment, with kindness and compassion; I betroth myself to You with faith, and you shall know Adonai." The verse from Hosea reminds me there are other metaphors for our relationship with God. God is not only a Father or King; for Hosea, God is a faithful spouse who has not given up on His unfaithful lover.

"The *ketubah* (the Jewish wedding contract) is like a life insurance policy," my homiletics teacher once told us. "It is not such a romantic document, but far deeper than a momentary feeling, the *ketubah* says, 'I'm going to take care of you. I'm going to stick with you. On our wedding day when everything is amazing and beautiful, I promise you that when we are angry and in pain, my love won't end.' That," he said, "is the love of the *ketubah*." That is the love of God I'm trying to hold on to this morning, because as I betroth myself to God, I am angry at Him too. I finish putting *tefillin* on and begin to pray looking out at waves.

I have always found myself drawn to water, playing on the edge of the endless ocean, watching and swimming in waves. Today, I hate them too. The waves and water continue, without end. They remind me that life does not pause but keeps going. Joel died. Yet I am here.

A Sephardic rabbi once told me the hardest moment of mourning is not when the body is lowered into the grave, nor when the earth makes its awful thud upon the coffin, nor even during *shiva* when everyone comes over and says foolish things that are meant to comfort. He said it is when, after spending a full week inside the house, looking at pictures, receiving visitors, saying *kaddish* in a *minyan* that the community brings to your home every morning and evening; it is when, after all that, you take your first few steps into sunlight and watch a car go by and see children heading off to school.

It is then when it hurts the most. It is then that you feel so utterly confused, because it seemed to you that life would never be the same, that a great sundering had occurred in the fabric of the world, that something—*someone*—great was lost, yet the world seems not to care. I hate the ocean and its waves, because they, who were my refuge, in whom I went to play and think and feel at home, they do not stop, do not care that Joel is gone. I cannot believe that *shiva* is over. I cannot believe that *shloshim* is done. Surviving feels like a sin, like I have stolen something I do not deserve.

Over and over again, the waves rise up, curling, and gently crashing upon the shore, stirring up sand and silt only for it to settle again. Beyond the sandy dunes held in place by grasses swaying in the breeze, I watch clouds blow ashore and showers wash clean the land. Then the sun comes out again. I praise God with His psalms and I read how "He heals the broken-hearted and binds up their wounds; He counts the number of the stars and calls them all by their names" (Psalm 147). I read, and I curse God's healing, because I do not want to heal, do not want to move on, do not want to forget Joel. I do not want for the memory of his loss to hurt less, for the songs we sang together at the piano in my living room to fade.

I stop my prayers and study the psalmist, whom I think I understand better now. What does the first part of the verse have in common with what follows? What is the connection between healing the broken-hearted and numbering the stars and calling them by name? The psalmist believes that we will feel healing in our hearts when we understand that God is in control of the vastness of nature, that there is a plan for the numbered stars, which He knows by name, and for us, whom He surely knows by name, too. The psalmist wants us to look at the vastness of the stars and the sea and, in the order, to see God's hand, God's plan. God numbers the stars. He calls them by name. God knows. He is in control. That should comfort me.

But I hate God's stars and sea and waves these days, because I see in them too large a plan to understand, only unending time and the cruel question of what it all can mean, if anything. I do not understand why Joel had to die. I do not understand why I am alive. I do not understand why it matters if the waves roll in and roll out, endlessly crashing on the shores. Wherever I go—to the Pacific, to the Gulf of Mexico—waves keep crashing, churning up silt, turning rocks into sand, dragging the land unwillingly away and swallowing it up, out into the sea.

A month and a half ago, Heather finished *shiva*, walked into the sunlight, and saw the world had not stopped. Joel's children are back at school. They sit and learn arithmetic and study the Torah. What does that mean? Heather wears her wedding ring and walks the aisles of a local supermarket and buys diapers and cereal while Joel is dead. What does *that* mean?

God comforts the broken-hearted and binds up their wounds. . .but what if the comfort is pain? From where, then, shall my help come?

This is what I pray to God, for a moment, before His sea and waves. And then my prayers, too, move on.

7

Sunday, January 13, 2008

I am back home in Los Angeles now. I have prayed often and have mostly been met by silence. I believe God hears prayer, but rarely have I felt God answer me.

This weekend, a low-pressure storm front in the Pacific Northwest and a high-pressure front off the coast of Southern California bring great, big waves to the beaches from Los Angeles to San Diego. Ten and twelve-foot waves close a boardwalk at Ocean Beach because they're breaking over the pier. Heather and the boys come visit from their home in the San Fernando Valley, on the other side of the Sepulveda Pass. We rarely visit each other's homes during the week because traffic is so bad it takes too long to make it back and forth. But on Sundays, it is just a half hour drive, so they come to our home to spend the day together. Our kids—Alon, Benjamin and Ranon—are eight, six and nearly two years old now. Joel and Heather's kids—Coleman, Miles and Ellis—are eight, six, and two years old. When Heather and the boys arrive, I feel lured to take Alon and Coleman, the two eldest boys, to the beach while Heather and Jen stay behind with the younger ones. I want Coleman and Alon to see the huge waves crashing on the coast.

I know I want to go to a beach but, as we pack the car and drive south on Robertson Boulevard and west on I-10, I have not yet made up my mind where to go. Malibu in the north, where the waves are smaller but the beaches can be quieter and it's easier on parking; or Manhattan Beach Pier in the south, where parking is much harder but the sand beach is wide and the waves are huge, as big as you'll find in the Los Angeles area. The waves or the quiet? Manhattan Beach or Malibu? I find myself following the ramp as it exits 1–10 and gently descends to merge with cars flowing towards LAX Airport on I-405 South, toward Manhattan Beach. Waves.

Alon asks me to zoom in on the GPS so it will look like the car is moving faster on the screen. Coleman looks up from his video game and asks me when we will be there. I explain we are driving to a beach that is a bit farther away but that has bigger waves. "Oh good! I'm going to ride those waves. It's going to be great!" he says from the backseat.

"No. Coleman, these waves are too big even for me to ride today." Coleman and I had been to the beach together during the summer. He has seen me bodysurf large waves before. "The water is going to be freezing because it's winter and these waves are going to be huge. Yesterday, they had a surf contest at a special beach in Northern California called 'Mavericks' and the waves were 30 feet high! We're just going to *watch* these waves," I tell him.

"I'm going to ride them!" he repeats from the back seat. I decide to drop it.

We exit the highway and follow some surface streets until the ocean finally comes into view. "Look, boys, there's the ocean!"

Looking out from the back of the car, through the front window, down to the beach a quarter mile away, Coleman screams, "Those waves don't look big at all! We're gonna have such a good time! We're gonna ride them!" I let it go again. When he sees the waves and feels how cold the water is, I figure his enthusiasm will fade.

We drive down Manhattan Beach Avenue, past shops and restaurants, and pull into a very crowded parking lot. Several cars have turned around and are exiting, having given up the search for a spot, when I notice a couple walking to a car directly opposite the beach. They put their stuff in the trunk, get in, and pull out. A parking space!

There are 35 minutes left on the meter. I have two quarters—enough for another 30 minutes, giving us a little over an hour at the beach, but we need more time. A couple of young guys come back to their truck to get a few things before returning to the beach. I ask them if either has change for a dollar. One looks and says, "I only have two quarters," but then he adds, "I don't need these. Just go ahead and take them." We now have an hour and 35 minutes. Perfect.

We have a bag with sand toys, a "snack bag," a bag with towels, my bathing suit, and a change of clothes for each boy. I also have a Jewish book; I figure I will study while the guys play in the sand. Our stuff in hand, we go to the public bathroom to change. Alon didn't bring a swimsuit because he knew he is not swimming in water that cold. Coleman's swimsuit doesn't fit him, so he puts on a loose pair of pants and a t-shirt. I tell both boys they can get their clothes wet and we'll just change into dry, non-sandy clothes for the ride home. We leave the changing rooms, trek across the beach under the pier, and set out towels to lie on. Before I have even put everything down, Alon is digging and Coleman is running in circles in the damp sand near where the waves stop on the beach.

The huge waves we have come to see are breaking a couple hundred yards out. I watch surfers riding them in the distance. Some of the waves rise up off the water and break all at once with tremendous force, sending their splash high enough to reach the boardwalk of the Pier, 30 or 40 feet above the ocean's surface. Others, more favored by the surfers, break from right to left and allow them a long ride from side to side before they bail out and return to surf again. The white water from the first break line churns and rolls towards us until, just a few yards out, it meets the upslope of the beach, rises up, falls again, and washes ashore.

I lie down on my towel and open my book, Maimonides' *Laws of Prayer*, chapter 8. He begins, "Communal prayer is always heard. Even when there are transgressors among [the congregation], the Holy Blessing One does not reject the prayers of the many." I have come to expect this kind of piety from Jewish texts, but I am tired of it today. "Is *always* heard?" Always? Really? Thousands of people around the world prayed for Joel, yet here I am at the beach alone with his son and mine. We were a community. Communal prayer is *always* heard? Did Maimonides really live a life and never see the absurdity of what he wrote? Why put such certainty to paper?

I look up from my reading and see Coleman has stopped running in circles. He is standing now, looking down and laughing as the cold waters retreat from around his legs, back into the Pacific, gently tugging at his toes. I have a swimsuit on but am not really in the mood to get wet. I would rather just lie in the sun and catch up on some studying while Alon and Coleman play quietly or run around enjoying the freedom of the wide-open space. But with Coleman so close to the cold waters, I put my book down and decide to watch him from closer up so that, if he wanders too far into the water while it recedes between waves, I can call to him to come back before the next one breaks; or if he gets knocked down by a strong wave that makes its way to the shoreline where he is playing, I can get to him quickly.

I am standing now, half way between our towels and the water. Coleman sees where I am and wanders closer towards the water. A wave recedes and, during the lull, Coleman walks farther still onto moist sand that only seconds before was picked up, tossed around, carried to and fro, and dropped into its place by the retreating ocean. In a moment, the sand will be swept up again so I call, "Coleman, come back a bit," and move towards him.

He takes a few steps but it is not back enough. A wave breaks in front of him. I hurry forward and feel the shock of the cold water rising from my toes to my knees. I grab Coleman's hand and hold up his body by his arm as the water knocks him off his feet and soaks his pants up to his waist. I look down to see if he's okay; for a moment he looks shaken, still reeling from the cold and the power of the water's pull as it slides back into the sea. But then a huge grin comes across his face. "That was great!"

"Yeah, that was," I tell him. "Now, let's head back up to the sand. See if you can help Alon with his digging." Still holding his hand, I start to walk and give him a pull back up the shore.

"No, that was great! Let's do it again!" he says, and faces towards the incoming white water. The next wave knocks us around; I pull Coleman up and he looks up at me, "Yeah! Wow! We're riding the waves! This is great!" He reaches out, says, "Let's stay more!" and squeezes my hand.

I do not know how to write with certainty about what I felt when Coleman squeezed my hand. I cannot tell you it was true in some objective sense—nobody, even Maimonides, has access to certainty about God. But when Coleman squeezed my hand, I felt he was an angel—not a heavenly angel with wings, but an angel in the sense of its Hebrew word, *malach*. It means, literally, messenger. I felt that God knew me, knew my broken heart since Coleman's father left this world, knew that the beach and its waves used to be places I went to for healing and understanding and that, from a deck in Mendocino and a patio in Galveston, they had become a source of pain for me. "If the comfort is pain, from where shall my help come?" I prayed.

Underneath the sun, standing in waves with Coleman's hand squeezing mine, as his father's hand could not just two months ago, I felt that God answered me. He had brought me to see something I could not have seen myself: that a boy with no father can still smile, that Coleman could laugh and play and love the world again, that hope and tomorrow and sweetness and light still abound in a world that had grown dark for me.

I felt in one moment that a low-pressure front and a high-pressure front; and great, big waves; and a visit from Heather and the boys; and a parking space at the beach; and quarters from a stranger; and Coleman, who would not suffer to play in the sand and so dragged me to the waves to stay and play and laugh under God's sun; that all this was given to show me what I could not see for myself. I felt gratitude overwhelm me like waves washing on the shore. I felt showered in God's light, and I squeezed Coleman's hand, brushed the soft blond hair he got from his mother, and told him, "Sounds good, Coleman, let's play a while."

8

Sunday, January 20, 2008. Body Memory

I have a massage this morning. The masseuse's hands rub quickly and lightly over my back for a while, "to warm up your muscles," she explains, after which she begins to press. First her fingers, then her palms, and finally her elbows push deeper and deeper into my shoulder blade, uncovering small knots, running them up towards my neck, pressing until they let go and seem to fade away. After I stood there with Coleman in the water, I thought I was getting better, beginning to heal. Her hands sense a secret far beneath my skin: "You carry pain in your shoulders," she says, and as she presses and rubs beneath the quiet flute music and faded light, I think about my body and how it is a repository for pain—and memory.

I return home. An hour later, Heather and the boys make another Sunday visit. The boys pile out of the minivan, say a quick hello, and bound into Alon and Benjamin's room at the front of the house. Alon and Benjamin take a new interest in their own toys now that Miles and Coleman are here. Both sets of brothers seem excited to be playing with someone besides one another. Jen and I greet Heather at the minivan and help her carry things inside. Instead of wandering further into the house with them, I linger in the boys' room and plant myself in the midst of the focused play.

My presence in the room is quickly noted, toys are set aside and a game of "pile on Rabbi Dan!" begins. Miles and Coleman jump on my back and push me like a tree to the ground in a pile of tickling and screaming, "Get Rabbi Dan!" Miles laughs and pushes against my back. As I feel his soft blond hair against the back of my neck, I think of how, the morning Joel died, I whispered to him a promise to take care of Miles. I stop resisting and allow myself to be tackled to the ground, lie still and, as they tickle and push, I shrink into myself and feel like an imposter: I cannot replace their father.

As they poke and prod me, I return to the pushing and tussling, but my mind wanders. Joel died in his hospital room, and, down the hall an hour later, Heather sat on the floor in the Witkin Meditation Room and told her sons under whom I now lay that their dad died. I remember Miles would not cry. I remember how he pushed his body into hers as if testing whether every dependable solid object in his world would just collapse—a hypothesis worth testing. The masseuse told me my body carries pain, but Miles' body on mine reminds me it carries not only stress in my shoulders; it carries memory all over.

I feel grateful, too, even as I think about Joel's death. I am grateful Miles can play again. I feel honored, and humbled, that I can be for Miles an older, adult male figure with whom he feels safe wrestling and laughing. But then I think back to the promise I made to Joel just minutes before he died, to help him let go of this world and journey to the next: "I will take care of the boys and Heather, my friend," I whispered into his ear as the ventilator forced air into his lungs. "We will take care of them. I love you." And I feel a tremendous sense of guilt and shame, because I cannot keep my promise.

Later in the afternoon, Heather and the boys will go to their own home and, while I am here to wrestle with Coleman and Miles now, I will put my own children to sleep, not his. I will neither soothe their tears, nor be a wall to lean upon when they wake up crying in the middle of the night. Did I lie to Joel on his deathbed? Did I deceive him into dying? What right do I have to wrestle with Miles, to give him a few temporary moments, when I cannot not give him what he deserves: a father?

For a moment, too, I yearn for, and understand for the first time, the idea behind the biblical institution of the Levirate marriage. Deuteronomy 25:5 says, "If brothers live together, and one of them dies, and has no child, the wife of the dead shall not marry outside to a stranger; her husband's brother shall go in to her, and take her to him for a wife, and perform the duty of a husband's brother to her. And it shall be that the firstborn which she bears shall succeed to the name of his brother who is dead, that his name be not put out of Israel."

Of course the analogy is not perfect. Joel and I were not blood brothers, but he was my brother. Joel was not without children; he had three sons. But the instinct that a brother would marry his brother's wife seems to me not just so that his name will live on, but so that his family will be taken care of. Like the promise I made to Joel.

9

Dr. Giller's Office at American Jewish University

American Jewish University (AJU) is a small liberal arts college with a number of graduate programs (including the Ziegler School of Rabbinic Studies where I was ordained) and a large department of continuing education. Its main campus sits atop the Santa Monica mountains between the west side of Los Angeles and the San Fernando Valley, just off the I-405 freeway. Ramah's offices are located there. Ever since I started rabbinical school in 1997, I have made the drive nearly every weekday on I-405 north, to the exit for the university at Mulholland Drive, either to attend classes as a student or to go to work.

Dr. Pinchas Giller is a quirky professor of *kabbalah* and mysticism at AJU. His classes in rabbinical school meander—one takes the courses as much for Dr. Giller as for the material he is teaching. He has an acute wisdom about the world one might expect from someone who lives in ancient texts. I don't plan to talk with him about what's happening to me, but one day I bump into him in the hall. We are both carrying our food from the cafeteria, and I decide to ask him if he has a moment. His office is dark and cramped. Books overflow their shelves.

I sit down in a chair opposite his desk and the words spill out. I tell him about wrestling with the boys. I tell him how I cannot play piano without crying because Joel used to play the keys I touch. I tell him about when I went running in Phoenix and how far away I feel from the swimmer I was in my youth. I tell him that when I take a shower and rub soap into my chest, I notice how it cleanses because it rubs and scrapes away decay. I see my wife's hair that gathers in the drain, caught in the strainer, and think about how it is dead. I clip my nails in the shower, and think about them as the part of my body that has died today.

I am 36-years-old and all I can focus on is that my body is sliding towards death. That is all I am: dying, dying, dying. We fight futilely to be clean and young, but really, we all are dying, slowly. "Rabbi Eliezer said, 'repent one day before you die'" (Pirkei Avot 2:15). Later, the Talmud asks, "Does a person then know when he shall die? Therefore you should repent today; perhaps tomorrow you will die. You will then find that all your days are spent with *tshuva*." (Shabbat 153a). All my days in *tshuva*— repentance. All my days dying.

"You have body memory," Dr. Giller counsels, echoing the words of the masseuse. "You need to try and stay away from that." He is warning me that one can mourn too much. Jewish tradition requires mourners to cover mirrors at the time of death because one can self-reflect too much. Mirrors are mesmerizing; one can gaze too long and get caught up in a whirlpool from which one does not escape. Some questions cannot be answered; they simply drive you mad.

"But I cannot get out of my body," I tell him. I carry Joel with me, like I carry my chest upon my torso.

"I know," he says patiently. "But be careful. You need to try and move on."

I feel I am gazing at the mirrors too long, but I cannot look away.

10

Ramah Office, American Jewish University

When I tell people I run Camp Ramah in California, they invariably ask, "Is that something you do all year long, or just during the summer?" They don't mean to be insulting; it's just that most people don't understand how much effort goes into running a summer camp. We also run programs and rentals all year round, but, even if we didn't, running the summer camp would be plenty of work for the entire year. My job entails the recruitment and registration of the 1,300 campers who attend the California camp; overseeing and managing a 15-person, year-round staff at our administrative offices in Los Angeles and at our camp in Ojai; raising funds for scholarships and capital projects; evaluating and preparing the recreational and educational aspects of our program; and hiring more than 250 young adult staff members who teach and inspire the campers in our care. Those are just a few of the things that fill my days from summer to summer. This is what occupies my time; I must mourn while life moves on.

One of my favorite parts of the job takes place in January and February, when we interview approximately 90 eleventh graders who have grown up at our camp and want to be counselors-in-training for the following summer. Many of the questions focus on the ins-and-outs of being a good counselor—being patient and compassionate, being good Jewish role models, working well as part of a team, those sorts of things. But as a rabbi, I also try to use the interview as an opportunity to encourage these young adults to reflect on their faith and what Judaism and God mean to them personally, and not just what they've been taught by someone else.

A young woman sits across from me. She is not one of the "perky" kids who are dressed fashionably and carry light conversations easily. She is darker, dressed in clothes purposely ripped; she does not wear make-up as if to say, "I am not interested in conforming." She is not angry, but piercing in honesty. She answers the regular questions well, and we are almost at the end of her interview time. I lean forward and ask, "If you could ask God one question, what would it be?"

"I don't even know if I believe in God," she says.

"Just play along," I persist. Sometimes I ask a question because I feel a person I am counseling needs to hear him or herself answer it. This time, it is I who wants to know.

"Why?" she says. The question hangs in the air. "That's it." She sits quietly staring across from me.

I respect the silence between us for a few moments, but in my mind, I think, "That's not it. Let me fill it in for you. 'Why have You created a world of such pain? Why am I here? Why the world? Why are You so absent and distant and cruel?' These are the questions I ask in the silence behind my eyes before I thank her for her answers and she leaves the room.

11

February 16, 2008. Camp Ramah, Ojai, CA

I am on a Winter Weekend, only a year or so after the weekend when Joel was here, pale and gray, and we thought he had a cold. I lead some of the prayers, tell some stories, and sing the blessings with the children who, at times, are able to draw a smile out of me. But most of what I do is an effort, pushing through a dull grayness. On weekends like this, sometimes I do a question-and-answer session with the campers or staff. Not today. What would I say if they asked me about God, or why good people suffer? What would I say if they asked me, "What do you believe, Rabbi Dan?" Would I tell them that God kills good people?

I pray this afternoon at the outdoor synagogue where Joel used to sing and make children happy. Later, I give a tour of camp, and we arrive at the tree house. I want to tell the families, "This is where Joel and I camped one night with our children before he got cancer and died." But I lie instead and tell them that it is a beautiful tree house where the youngest campers enjoy their first overnight campout.

12

Tuesday morning, February 19, 2008. Home

An *upsherin* is, admittedly, a strange ceremony. Families and friends gather when a Jewish boy turns three and celebrate his first haircut. The custom of growing out a boy's hair until his third birthday is just that, a custom. It is a beautiful one, but not often observed, and therefore unfamiliar to many Jews. We did not have an *upsherin* for our eldest son, Alon. We tried. We let his hair grow out for as long as we could, but two years later, after his younger brother, Benjamin, was born, we found large clumps of Alon's hair under his crib in the morning. He had pulled it out during the night, presumably out of anxiety from having a little brother with whom to share and compete for *abba* and *imma's* attention. So we cut it and tried to soothe his anxiety. We spent extra time with him, hoping to show him our hearts did not have a limited amount of love, but had grown and could love him infinitely, and his new brother too.

Our middle son, Benjamin, didn't have a younger brother to worry about in his first three years; he made it to his *upsherin* with his hair curly, big, and blond; he looked like a cherub until the day we cut it off. Our youngest son, Ranon, is two years old. His hair is long, golden blond with ringlets that flow below his shoulders; it is the envy of women everywhere we go.

It is 5:45 AM and I have the early shift. Over the past many weeks, I wake up and sit with Ranon in the stillness of his room. I read him stories, his little body curled up in my lap. I walk him to the kitchen, lift him up and place him precariously on the counter. His feet dangle over the edge while I walk to the other side of the kitchen, take the coffee grinder down from where it is stored and look over at him. He watches me, aware of the height, knowing not to move: to fall from this high would not be fun. I don't know why I do this. I feel proud of him for knowing, at two years old, the difference between when you can squirm and when you must be still, for knowing where the limits are. I did this with my older two sons; neither ever fell. I doubt myself sometimes, as a person and a father, and wonder if somehow I *want* to place them in harm's way, to prepare them with small moments of pain for the larger anguish that awaits us all.

Ranon pushes the button on the coffee grinder, and his face lights up at the sudden whir of blades finely cutting beans, throwing them wildly about the canister. He holds the button for a few seconds. "Okay, that's enough," I say, and he lets go. Ranon sits patiently while I empty the grinds into the copper mesh filter, pour a cup and a half of water in the corner of the maker, flip "brew," and press the "1–3 cups" button. When I'm finished, Ranon says, "di da?" He is asking for a gummy bear vitamin. I give him one from the basket on the counter and lower him to the floor.

We hold hands and walk together down the hall and out the front door of our home. Our feet are chilled from the cold ground as he collects the newspaper from the end of our driveway and proudly carries his prize back towards the house. Under the wide sky beneath light from a sun that has not yet risen, I gather him up and hold him close, his cheek next to mine. Feeling Ranon's small, warm body wrapped in soft pajamas next to mine, I think of how Joel cannot hold his children in the early morning any more, which, when he lay sick in the hospital, is what he said he missed most.

When Joel talked in the hospital about missing his kids, a part of me thought stupidly about how much work children are, about how they are a distraction from reading and writing and praying, about how I secretly treasure going on a business trip, because I am able to have time for myself. It is incredible to me that it even arose in my mind that Joel was somehow lucky because he was sick and was given so many uninterrupted months to study and write. Of course, all along, he was too weak to read.

Ranon's full name is Ranon Jay; Jay's parents and brother were honored that we wanted to name our third child in his memory. Ranon's name means a lot to me, but it hurts too. Jewish tradition in Ashkenazi families (families descended from the medieval Jewish communities along the Rhine river in Germany) is to name after close relatives who have died, such as grandparents. Between our own children and the children of our siblings, we were blessed already to have given a name that will continue the memory of each of those grandparents from the generation that came before. When Jennifer was pregnant with Ranon, we faced the daunting task of choosing a first and middle name with few constraints, other than knowing that Ranon was going to be a boy.

Without grandparents' names to guide us or even give us initials with which to begin, we played around with many ideas until we arrived at "Ranon Jay," or in Hebrew, "Ranon Ya'akov." The first name, Ranon, means "to give a ringing cry," usually with joy. It is taken in part from the verse that opens Psalm 96 of the Friday night service each week— "*Lechu n'ranena l'Adonai*"—"let us go and sing with joy to Adonai." Ranon, from *n'ranena*, to sing with joy. But, at first hearing, Ranon Jay is an oxymoron—a juxtaposition of two ideas that don't go together. Because Jay suffered for so much of his life.

I remember an email he sent to me from the hospital bed in his home while I was in Israel in October of 1995. He wrote,

> Hmmm…I didn't go to services this year. After all, last year I struggled to get there and prayed my butt all the way down to 96 pounds, and look what it got me. Not a wonderful year. So this time I'm letting God go at it without me. I know the story of Job, but I can't do it anymore. When I got the job in London, I thought that was the reward for everything I've gone through since I was twelve. That opportunity essentially just fell into my lap, but only because I finished college in December. Wrong again.

Ranon and I come inside and sit on the couch in the living room near the piano. I think strange thoughts. Joel would play and we both would sing. Jay, too, would play and we both would sing. I am afraid to play and sing with another friend, lest I curse them with cancer and death. When I play and sing alone, sometimes I hope God will send me to join them and end the sadness. Death by music.

Joel at least had children who carry his music and face, his hair and hands into the world. I think of Jay who died a few months after I married. In Genesis, there is such a contrast between those who have children, and those who have none. In Genesis chapter 11, there is a long list of our ancestors who had children and died only in old age—Shem, Arphaxad, Salah, Eber, Peleg, Reu, Serug, Nachor and Terah. All had sons and daughters and lived for many years. Then it says, quite suddenly, Terah's son, Abram (later to be renamed "Abraham"), married Sarai (later to be renamed "Sarah"), "*but Sarai was barren; she had no children*" (Genesis 11:30).

Barren. No child. Barren means she couldn't have children, so why repeat the idea—"she had no children"? The redundancy, we are told, points to Sarai's despair—she experiences her own barrenness, but she also experiences the absence of children *not born*.

I think of how Jay had *no* children to carry on his face and hands, his music and love, for he died too soon, before the prime of his life. I do not know why I am allowed to sit with Ranon this morning while Joel and Jay cannot; to think I deserve it when they did not sickens me, seems an obscenity. I refuse to believe I deserve to live, and so living is a puzzle for me now.

The question of my dead friends and their lives *not* lived, the absence of their lives that I carry inside my life, fills me up. They are present in their absence; they are, *not here*. Three months since Joel slipped away from me, almost twelve years after my friends and I drove away from the grave where Jay lays buried in Northern Virginia, I cannot stop a river of tears that overflows at strange, sometimes inappropriate, moments of the day. It is a dark well, a mystery I feel more deeply, not less, as time goes by.

The coffee is ready. While I pour a cup, Ranon lies down on his back on the smooth hardwood floor. He wants me to spin him. His pajamas make it easy to use one of his legs to twirl him around and around, slowly at first, then he giggles with joy and asks for more. As I spin him again, faster this time, I ask myself, "is the world all darkness with moments of joy, or all joy with moments of darkness?"

In the Talmud (Eruvin 13b) we learn that for two and a half years, the schools of Shammai and Hillel argued. Shammai argued it would have been better if human beings were never created. Hillel argued it is better that we were. They finally took a vote and decided (quite unusually in the Talmud) in favor of the house of Shammai: It would have been better if human beings were *not* created, but now that we were, we should investigate our deeds—past or future.

I understand that last part to mean: now that we are here, we should think about where we've been and where we're going. We should live with purpose. But I love the rabbis for the first answer. Sometimes they make more sense to me than God. Not because they are wiser, but because they answer me as a human being. They admit it. They stare straight into the darkness that surrounds us, into the veil of the world that constantly covers death beneath every surface. They do not hide behind platitudes. For two and half years, they called out the terrifying reality of this life, cried out against the unknowable question of suffering, the inescapable mystery, and declared to the heavens and history, "It is true! Attention must be paid to cries, prayers and tears that are never answered! It would have been better if human beings never were!"

That is the pain of grief. It is the shudder of terror I felt when I was running on the streets in Phoenix—when I thought about my body and its decay, and how all we are is dying; when I thought about my children and cried out: "What have I done to bring them into a world that is only dying?" I love them so much, and there is nothing I can do to protect them. Would it have been better not to bring them into this world? Was my act of procreation not a blessing but a cruelty? But the rabbis knew: no such choice is given. Suicide, while a temptation, is an abomination, though I worry less these days about God's reaction than the wreckage it leaves in its wake for others, for children and spouses and friends who grieve without end. I love the rabbis because for two and a half years they debated, and in their conclusion they sent me a message: you are not alone when you think this way and feel what you feel, so sad and lost.

13

Rabbi Artson's Office, Monday, March 3rd

Arguments about God and suffering have existed for centuries and can be summarized as follows: If God is all-good, and all-powerful, and all-knowing, the presence of real evil cannot be accounted for. All theologies wiggle their way out of this conundrum by denying either one of these points or the reality of the evil.

Rabbi Brad Artson is the dean of the Ziegler School. His office is just a few doors down from mine at AJU. Rabbi Artson, too, was Joel's friend. He is a man of deep wisdom and faith, and I sit outside his office waiting for my appointment, seeking answers.

We are reading the Book of Exodus at this time of year. It is comforting that God saves His people in distress but not always easy to believe. For a time in the desert, the Israelites are free from slavery, but they are understandably bewildered, untrusting that it is a benevolent (all-good) God who has saved them. Now, on the other side of the Red Sea, they are thirsty and cry out against Moses, God's servant, "Why have you brought us up out of Egypt, to kill us and our children and our cattle with thirst?" The question may seem improper, ungrateful, like something an entitled teenager might ask when all a parent is trying to do is help. But is it so unreasonable a question?

Sure, the Jewish people are happy to be free from Pharaoh, but one could ask of this all-good God Who saved them: Why did You wait for so long? If I stipulate that You are all-powerful, why in God's name did You leave us there for hundreds of years? When Pharaoh fears the Jewish people "will become too numerous and, in a time of war, they may join our enemies and wage war against us and go up from the land," his solution is curiously to have them build "storage cities for Pharaoh, Pithom, and Raamses" (Exodus 1:10–11).

Building seems a strange "solution" to the problem of too many children. Some *midrashim*—classical stories from the Jewish tradition that embellish and fill in gaps from the Bible—attempt to explain the link between building and overpopulation: they illustrate the horror of Pharaoh's "solution" by imagining that children were buried in the bricks, that their bodies were used for mortar. Yes, God saved the Jewish people, but is it so unreasonable to cry out, "Our babies! They crushed our babies before our very eyes! Where have You been?" Is it so unreasonable to ask whether God is all-good?

The story of the Exodus is foretold in the Book of Genesis—God indeed is all-knowing. God says to Abraham years before: "Know for certain that your descendants will be strangers in a country not their own, and they will be enslaved and mistreated for 400 years" (Genesis 15:13). Why does God do this? Apparently to make God's name great, to show how (all) powerful He is. He even tells Pharaoh this is why He created him in the first place, just to make His name great: "Indeed, for this very cause have I raised you up—to show my power through you and so that my name will be declared through the world" (Exodus 9:16).

Is it so unreasonable to ask God: "You knew a long time ago we would be enslaved there, even knew it would be for 400 years! Wasn't it You who created a famine to force Jacob and his family to settle there? Wasn't it You who forced the new Pharaoh to forget Joseph, who planted the fear inside him that we would grow to be too large a people, who stoked his fear and gave him the whip he used to hurt us so long? Where have You been? Did the ends justify the means? Was it worth the babies still in the bricks just to save us and make Your name great?" I read the story this year and wonder if God's name is so great after all, and whether it should inspire my continuing loyalty.

Later in the desert, God is frustrated with the Jewish people, as any parent is with a disobedient child. When we make a golden calf, He threatens to kill us and start over again with Moses, but Moses convinces Him not to. How? Moses tells him that if God kills us, everyone will say that God is evil. "Why should the Egyptians say, 'It was with evil intent that He brought them out to slay them in the mountains, and to wipe them off the face of the earth'?" (Exodus 32:12) They will say these things about God, Moses worries. I understand his concern.

Jews have a long history of wondering about the goodness of God. If God is like a parent, one can argue that a good parent lets her children stumble to help them grow. If children start to fight, they have to learn to work it out for themselves. But if you are in the kitchen, and, through the window, you see one son pick up a baseball bat and start killing the other, and you do nothing, we have a word for that: neglectful abuse.

When the rabbis asked how it is that God could have allowed Cain to kill Abel, they compare the scene to when Caesar put two gladiators into a ring for sport and let them fight it out to the death. They compared God to Caesar. Elie Wiesel wrote a play about a group of Hasidim in Auschwitz who put God on trial, found him guilty, and then went to pray. When asked in 2008 if the story was apocryphal, Wiesel replied, "I was there. . ."

While I'm waiting for Rabbi Artson to finish with the appointment before mine, I re-read the letter he wrote to the Ziegler community to help them in the struggle to understand God in the wake of Joel's death.

Dear Ones:

I was moved and impressed (as I always am) by the seriousness and honesty with which you are confronting your feelings in the wake of tragedy. I'm going to offer you a somewhat different context than some of my colleagues and friends might offer. My perspective is deeply shaped by the [philosophical approach called] "process thought" that I've been wrestling with for the past year.

[What does "process thought" teach me?]. . .I believe that God, in choosing to create, created us really. That means that our independence is not illusory or ephemeral. We, along with all creation, have real agency, and the choices we make are truly untrammeled, unprogrammed, and unforeseen by God. God is vulnerable to surprise, disappointment just as we are. The universe unfolds according to its own inner logic, the laws of physics operate and God cannot/does not suspend them based on some moral standards. As Rabbi Harold Kushner says, asking the universe to treat you better because you are moral is like expecting the bull not to charge because you are a vegetarian. I believe that God did irrevocable *tzimtzum* (withdrawal), creating the reality of our own autonomy and agency, along with all creation.

I believe that people misunderstand the nature of divine "power" as coercive, as omnipotence, which I regard as a philosophical mistake, a religious disaster, and a source of emotional and ethical torment. Thinking of God as having all the power leaves us rightly feeling betrayed and abandoned ("was I not good enough for God to intervene?"). It leaves theologians in the position of Job's friends - discounting our core ethical knowledge in an attempt to defend the indefensible. We do know good and evil; we are infused with that awareness by God. And Joel dying young is indefensible, especially if God is omnipotent. Hiding behind "it's a mystery" or "we can't understand" or "it's all for the best" is (in my humble opinion) worse than unsatisfying, because it requires either blaming the victim (in this case, Joel and us) or denying our ethical compass.

I don't think you have to abandon a conviction of a loving God. But I invite you to grow past an almighty one. If God has truly ceded to creation the ability to make choices, then God didn't kill Joel, and looking for God in special effects mistakes theater or science fiction for life. . .I saw God being very busy throughout Joel's struggle - in moments of laughter and song, in the strength of the relating that bound us all as a community and kept Joel feeling connected through his very last minutes, in the determination to be there with and for his family throughout and beyond the ordeal. I never expected God to guarantee an outcome or suspend the natural. I did expect to find God in the steady constant lure toward good choices and responsibility. And in that God did not disappoint.

But I am not ready to internalize the letter, its meaning, its significance. Not yet. And so I sit in Rabbi Artson's office and cry. I tell him how my prayer life has run dry, how God is to me a distant mystery now, how I cannot reach out for comfort to One who kills. I tell him that, for the first time since I found God thirteen years ago in Israel, I feel like my relationship with Him is slipping away, that I don't know upon what I will base my life, but that believing in, much less praying to, God is an exercise in pain. I feel the temptation of Elisha ben Abuya, the rabbi who stared at a child lying dead on the ground, declared "There is no judgment; there is no Judge," and walked away.

I am afraid of starting my life over again, of returning to the void at the center of everything and trying to build my life anew, all the while knowing death will come sooner or later. I am afraid of letting go of all the learning and knowledge and love I have found in God and Torah and the Jewish tradition. But I am also afraid I will find the courage to do so. I wonder if I am questioning too much, that greater men endured more loss and blessed God as the True Judge, if my inability to heal is a sign of lack of faith. Am I fit to be a rabbi anymore? Perhaps I can be a Jew without being a rabbi but, I wonder, can I be a rabbi if I feel such anger towards God? I sit in his office looking for answers, like I sat in Dr. Giller's office on the same campus just a few weeks before, hoping he can bring me back, as if something he could say would make it all right again.

Rabbi Artson is patient and sits with me for a while. I know the theology will come, but he is wise enough not to force it upon me, to wait for me to ask, first and foremost to sit with me in my pain and communicate without words: you are not alone. When I finally ask him how to make sense of all this, he offers no standard, easy answers, but only shares his advice based upon conclusions he has drawn after many years of life and study, challenge and pain.

"You have to let go of this understanding of God," he counsels, calling upon the words from his letter while adding a personal, proactive call to action. "God is good, but He is not all-powerful. To believe in an all-powerful God is toxic," he says, directly but gently. He is inviting me to "grow past" thinking that God has all the power and that, therefore, God killed Joel. He is encouraging me to let my current image of God die and to let another one take its place, so my relationship with God can live again.

He is right, of course, that it is a toxic theology to try to pray for comfort to the One who killed. What's more, our tradition has other, more productive ways of understanding God than to say God gave Joel the cancer. What Rabbi Artson—and Rabbi Kushner before him—suggest is that one way our tradition solved the theological conundrum is by saying, "God is not all-knowing," or "God is not all-powerful." The rabbis of the Talmud taught, "the world goes according to its way," by which they meant that, in creating the world, God let go of controlling its every whim and turn and knowing in advance how everything will turn out. We, and the world, are really free, so God is not responsible for cancer, but instead can be found in the loving and community.

But I am stuck, stubborn. I have objections to Rabbi Artson's answers. If God's world "goes according to its way," then hasn't God cut Himself off from what happens to us? Doesn't that mean God cannot intervene? Why should I pray to such a distant, or hapless, God? And was such an initial choice—to cut Himself off from the world as it unfolds—ethical? Isn't God either irresponsible or cruel for creating a world of such suffering without remedy? And doesn't the *Amidah*, the thrice-daily prayer at the heart of Jewish liturgy, describe God as a "King who kills"? True, the prayer continues, "and brings to life and causes salvation to sprout," but kill He does.

Rabbi Artson's answer works for many people—I have seen it provide comfort to our community. It may help me some day, but I cannot accept his answer today. In his letter, he wrote that to believe God kills and is all-good causes us to "deny our moral compass." We are left not knowing whether what is good from our perspective in this world corresponds with what God says is good.

Isaiah taught, "My thoughts are not your thoughts, neither are My ways your ways" (Isaiah 55:8). God is all good-powerful-knowing, but the evil, which you perceive as evil, is not really evil. This leads to an intolerable, dizzying disorientation, one that Rabbi Artson denies because, he asks, "how can we try to serve God by doing what is good if we can't be sure what good is?" But I *am* disoriented, so my toxic theology has one advantage: it matches how I feel—dizzy, confused. "I know," Rabbi Artson says, and gives me a hug before I leave.

What my attempt at understanding God's role in suffering lacks in comfort, it makes up for in accuracy. God kills. He killed Jay. He killed Joel. I believe God is good. But I do not understand God. He disorients me, angers me, and will, in the end, kill me too. He is awesome, to be feared. And yet He is generous, to be loved. Courage is what I need now to get me through the days.

14

Purim

I do not feel like costumes and drinking this year. If I were an official mourner, Jewish law would require me to keep things low-key. It would be easier to just forget about it. Joy can't be forced. But I'm not officially a mourner, and we are known for our Purim party. Friends are expecting invitations. So we send out an Evite, watch the RSVPs come in and make preparations. Moon bounce for kids (and adults) in the backyard. Sodas. Beer. Salad and chips. The rabbis teach "there is no joy without meat and wine," so we order kosher fried chicken. Wine? Nope. Our friends know to bring scotch instead, lots of it.

Around 3:00 PM people begin to arrive. They say hello, hang up their coats, send their kids to the moon bounce and place their bottle of scotch (single malt only) onto the buffet in the dining room before getting some food. Ardbeg. Armore. Bowmore. Dalwhinnie. Glenfiddich. The Glenlivet. Glenmorangie. Highland Park. Lagavulin. Laphroaig. Oban. A bottle of Johnnie Walker Black sits sadly in the corner, clearly brought by a newbie. The Talmud also teaches, "When wine goes in, the truth comes out." So I decide to embrace the *mitzvah* and see what will emerge. This could be interesting.

People are eating and talking. I have a glass of Oban in one hand and am carrying the bottle in the other. I walk around filling people's glasses, drinking *l'chaims* with each one. After a while, I decide to slow down and head over to the moon bounce where my presence makes a big splash with the kids. Scotch and bouncing seems like a bad idea after a while, so I get off and head inside.

A solid group of scotch connoisseurs has gathered around the buffet. I grab the Ardbeg, fill glasses, and a round of toasts begins. Someone toasts to life and health. We drink. Someone else toasts to the Jewish people. We drink. We sing a Purim drinking song in honor of "Charvona," a eunuch in the Book of Esther who, when Haman gets caught, suggests to King Achashverosh that he hang Haman on the tree he had prepared for Mordecai. "Also remember Charvona for good!" we sing aloud for a while. Then we drink again.

The singing dies down. "*D'var Torah*," someone calls out. "Some words of Torah from the host." Eyes turn to me. I take a deep breath and recount a teaching by Rabbi Yitzchak Hutner I learned many years ago.

> The Jewish lunar year is only 354 days long, so seven times every nineteen years, a leap month—a second instance of the month of Adar—is added to keep Passover in the spring. Rabbi Hutner points out that, according to the Jewish lunar calendar, Purim must be celebrated in the month of Adar, but in leap years, Purim could be celebrated in either Adar 1 or Adar 2. Why is it celebrated in Adar 2? Rabbi Hutner argues that it is to juxtapose two stories about how the Jewish people were saved, each of which helps us to know God in different ways: the story of Purim and the story of Passover. Passover, he says, is like a flashlight one can use to find his friend in a dark room. Passover is a holiday when God's presence was undeniable. "A common woman at the [Red] Sea saw God more clearly than any of the prophets did," says the *midrash*. Plagues. Seas. Pillars of fire. God has arrived. A flashlight in a dark room clearly lighting the way towards redemption.
>
> But on Purim, adds Rabbi Hutner, there is no flashlight. God's name is completely absent from the Book of Esther in which the story of Purim is told. On Purim, we find our friend "through any sense other than that which can be seen or proven." The room is dark and it remains dark—you cannot prove to me that God is there. Darkness surrounds us; destruction is all around. We grope and feel nothing. We cry out, and no one answers. Finally in de-spair, we sit and cry and grow quiet and still. In that darkness and pain and through our brokenness and tears, a voice echoes. We are unsure where it is from, cannot prove it is even there at all, but it says quietly: "I am here. You are not alone." That is Purim—and that, too, teaches Rabbi Hutner, is a way to know God.
>
> My friends, I prefer Purim to Passover. I do not live in a world of plagues and seas and miracles so plainly seen. I live in a world of darkness where I cry out and there is no answer. I cannot see that God is here any longer.

Nobody moves. People look around awkwardly. Bill asks for every-one's attention. "I have a toast," he says. "To fallen friends." Glasses are raised. "We miss you. You are not forgotten." We keep our glasses high. A silence hangs in the air.

"Amen," I say.

"Amen," the room repeats. I lower my glass and take a deep drink to the bottom. I hold the scotch in my mouth, feel the tingling on my cheeks and tongue. After a moment, I swallow, and feel the burn as it goes down. People start to eat again. A hum of chatter returns to the room.

15

Peet's Coffee

I am a rabbi wearing green on St. Patrick's Day. At Peet's Coffee on Beverly Boulevard, I am trying to force myself to write again. I sit down at the computer, look for a few moments at Freecell, and feel the urge to click and "challenge" myself to a game; a way to avoid the terror of a blank screen.

Last night, I spoke to Heather. She gave me strength, not in what she said, but in hearing her voice. It helps to know she understands. Of course she understands; she feels more deeply the ache and hollow emptiness that is all around, like God is supposed to be. Everywhere absence and void.

Hanukkah was a forced exercise for the kids. Putting on *tefillin* in Phoenix felt foreign, so I went for a run but carried Joel with me in my chest. I continue to pray, to send words upward, but they fall flat, echoes in the air before me. I sat with Rabbi Artson and Dr. Giller, sought wisdom from them and the Jewish tradition. God remains a mystery, distant, illusive. I celebrated Purim. Still, the pain endures. I am not officially a mourner. I hide my sorrow from the community so as not to intrude upon the sadness of those who "really" grieve. I hold a *kaddish* prayer within, responding to others' prayers, not offering my own. Jewish law gave meaning to my life but also betrays me, casts me out. Yet. . .

Even without the mourning rituals, looking back, I see I have found a different path to mourn. The structure of Jewish life—the regularity of daily prayer, study, even the rhythm of the holiday seasons—these things remain. They are vessels that contain me. They provide no answers, but give me a framework, at least, for asking questions.

After I went to the beach and saw Coleman playing in the waves, part of me thought I was done. I thought that experience meant that I had turned a corner, that in feeling God's presence in the squeeze of Coleman's hand, I would move forward with a sense of closure and healing. But it was only a moment, a holy memory. It did not endure. The masseuse revealed a secret my body could not conceal: mourning ebbs and flows like the sea, churns me up inside and recedes like waves along the sandy shore. It is never done.

After his perilous journey in *The Lord of the Rings*, Frodo Baggins returns to his home in the Shire he set out to save, but realizes he will never feel at home again. "How do you pick up the threads of an old life?" he asks. "How do you go on, when in your heart you begin to understand? There is no going back. There are some things that time cannot mend. Some hurts that go too deep. That have taken hold." My friends are gone. I will carry them with me, changed forever, never whole as before.

chapter 5

And Back Again

Elie Wiesel once wrote, "I was angry at God too, at the God of Abraham, Isaac, and Jacob: How could He have abandoned His people just at the moment when they needed Him?" It is an important, yet little known fact, that Elie Wiesel studies Talmud every day, and has done so most of his life.

1

Camp Ramah, Ojai, CA.

IT IS APRIL 2008. I am at Ramah for Passover again. Heather and the boys are not here. An angel in the Jewish community gave money to send them on a much-needed Passover vacation to London to meet Deborah, who flew to meet them from Israel. Joel is present in his absence; most people in the community are aware that his loss is a personal one for me. They do not ask; rather Joel hovers as a topic felt but unspoken.

On Seder night, I eat matzah and refrain from leavened bread. I attend services the next morning and sing Hallel—the special celebratory psalms—and remember my eyes meeting Joel's just one year ago. I place my tallit over my head and am surrounded by white cloth, bathed in light. The sun shines through large sliding doors that open onto the grassy hill in the center of camp. As the congregation passionately chants, "The dead shall not praise You, nor those who descend in silence, but we shall bless You from now and forever more" (Psalm 115:16), tears well up in my eyes. "The dead shall not praise You." I wipe tears away with my tallit and lower it onto my shoulders as Hallel ends. I observe the festival but cannot celebrate.

Why? Of course I miss Joel. I mourn his absence at camp. But I realize an additional problem is the challenge of Passover itself. On no holiday are we instructed to believe God participates in our lives more palpably than on Passover. The Hagaddah teaches, "In every generation, each person must see himself as if he personally left Egypt." Seder night requires every Jew to believe God has personally redeemed him—a belief that, this year especially, is hard.

The story of Passover is the story of God who heard His people's cries, of God who cared enough to alter nature's course and perform miracles to save His chosen people. Such a vision of God feels foreign to me, not only in the wake of Joel's death, but because we face a challenge to our faith unique in the history of the Jewish people: we live after the Shoah. If we affirm the uniqueness of the Shoah as a tragedy, an evil unlike any other in Jewish (much less human) history, we face an equally unique challenge: how can we authentically re-live the redeeming story of Passover just 60 years after the Shoah?

On Passover, God should feel present, but how do we believe in God's presence after a period when God was seemingly so absent? The purpose of the Exodus, teaches the Torah, is that we will "know that I, Adonai, am your God" (Exodus 6:7). But how are we to know God if, in the midst of our greatest despair, we cried out and He could not be found? I go on walks around camp with Ranon in the early mornings. I swim laps in the pool and lead the blessings at meals. I try to move through the festival; it is not moving me.

I feel blessed I was not the rabbi of a synagogue this year. If I were a congregational rabbi, I would have had to stand up on Friday nights and Saturday mornings and continue to teach Torah. I would have had to conduct funerals and weddings, to counsel and comfort people through their confusion and sadness. I have no idea how I would have done any of that, for it is I who has needed counsel and comfort, words of inspiration. I was spared.

But two days from now, on the last day of Passover, there is a tradition that the camp's rabbi gives a sermon before the Yizkor service in memory of those who have died. I cannot avoid speaking about Joel. For me, speaking is almost never impersonal. To speak at Yizkor, just five months after he died, just a year after he walked these very campgrounds on this very holiday, and not talk about his death would be, for me, bizarre, even obscene. But I don't know what to say. I have been trying to think of something since the festival began six days ago.

2

Yizkor

I wake up on the last morning of the festival and have nothing prepared. I pour myself a cup of coffee and, while Jen and the boys are at breakfast, I pull a book off the shelf, sit down on the porch and open it to one of my favorite essays, "On Self Reliance," by Ralph Waldo Emerson. The irony of looking to Emerson for wisdom is not lost on me. He says (though he would hate the fact that I quote him), "the highest merit we ascribe to Moses, Plato, and Milton is that they set at naught books and traditions, and spoke not what men, but what they thought."

I realize I have spent the past five months wandering, seeking everyone else's answers. I was sad, and scared of my sadness, of what it might reveal. Neither Rabbi Artson nor Dr. Giller nor other teachers and friends could help me find my way back. I was scared of solitude. In seeking counsel, I was avoiding the most difficult task: looking within.

This morning, I am not so naïve as to think I will manage to solve the problem of God and suffering that has plagued rabbis and the rest of us for centuries. But I need to find my answers, to grow beyond thinking what my teachers have taught me. In a few hours, the moment for the Yizkor service will arrive, and the congregation will look to me, not my teachers, for words of memory and comfort. I need to find my words, my approach, my own way through the darkness. I sometimes wonder if I took the job at Ramah instead of at a synagogue because I was afraid of a moment like this—that I would stand up before the congregation and my wisdom would run dry.

I sense, too, that, in this writer's block, not only one sermon is at stake; I feel that if I cannot articulate a way through this darkness, perhaps I do not really have one. I fear the anger that will not subside. Can I tell a family in pain, "God is all-powerful. God is all-knowing. And I dare not tell you the death of the innocent is good. It is not. So I believe God is not all-good. The psalms are wrong. God does not guard those who love Him." Can I quote them the second blessing of the Amidah, "God kills," if that is what I believe is true? I became a rabbi to help comfort and heal, not rub salt in a wound. Better not to speak at all than to wound with truth.

I wonder if I simply lack the insight others seem to possess or the faith they can profess. I think back to the night before Joel's funeral, and wonder how I will continue to build a life as a rabbi, to help people find their way if I cannot find my own? I take another book off the shelf and head in the direction of the chapel, not knowing if inspiration will come.

Above the chapel, to the side of the grassy hill, is an outdoor sanctuary called Kikar Zion, "Zion Square" (named after a central meeting place in downtown Jerusalem). During the summer, the entire camp gathers there on Friday night to welcome Shabbat together. This morning it is empty. Families finish breakfast in the dining room. Prayers will begin soon. I sit on a bench still damp from the morning dew and feel the warmth of the spring sun shine on my face.

"What did you say when you prayed a year ago?" I ask aloud. "How did you do it, Joel?" Birds chirp in the trees. One squirrel chases another up a tree. Joel was here a year ago. He did not stop believing. He celebrated Passover even though he himself had cancer. Joel's faith, like the Passover, challenges me. It is flashlight in a dark room. A gift. "Who am I," I ask myself, "to refuse to receive such a gift?"

Beside me on the bench is the book I grabbed when I left the house to come to services. It is a book of responsa—of questions and answers about Jewish law—written by Rabbi Ephraim Oshry. What is unique about these responsa is that they were asked and answered in the Kovno ghetto in Lithuania, in the midst of the Shoah. If those who lived through the Shoah could find the strength to ask what God required of them while they lived through hell, if Rabbi Oshry could find the strength to answer, who am I to lose faith when they did not?

People slowly leave the dining room and walk up the path to the chapel and the prayers begin. The Torah is read. More people arrive for Yizkor. The Torah is lifted, the reading of the haftarah—a selection of the prophets corresponding to the Torah reading—is concluded. The chapel is full. I stand up and take my place at the reader's table in the center of the room.

In college, I had a professor who used to tell us that, when we wanted to understand a phenomenon, we should ask ourselves: what would life be without it? If you wanted to understand the phenomenon of freedom, you had to think about a world without choice. If you wanted to understand communication, imagine a world without the possibility of connection between people.

Today is *Yizkor*, a day of memory. What would the world be without memory? One answer, perhaps surprising, is that it would be easier, more pleasant, less painful. To remember those who are not here is to call attention to their absence in the world. On the verse, "Jacob departed Be'er Sheva and went to Haran" (Genesis 28:10), the biblical commentator Rashi points out that the verse could have just as easily have said that Jacob went to Haran. "Why does it need to mention his departure from Be'er Sheva?" he asks. "When a righteous person leaves a place," Rashi answers, "it leaves an impression." Our loved ones made an impression. The more beloved a person, the more painful it is to remember they are gone.

I will say plainly what many of you have noticed: this Passover my experience of memory has been hard, and yes, painful. Last Passover, my friend, my student, and camp's former *Rosh Musica*, Joel Shickman, spent what would be his last days ever walking these holy grounds. Today is the first *Yizkor* service since his death last November. His memory is painful for me.

Earlier this week, my family did our annual trip to the Channel Islands just off the California coast. Last year, Joel and I did that trip together, with our boys. This year, the spring flowers were in bloom; the view of the ocean from the mountain ridge was breathtaking. But the hike, for me, was filled with loss. Joel was not with me. If only I could forget, I would not feel the searing pain still so raw in my soul. If only I could live in a world without memory, that world would hurt less than this one. I swim in memories that needle me, give me no rest. But I do not wish to forget, for memory is not only pain.

Memory is sweet too. I remember talking with Joel at the tree house while our children lay in their sleeping bags under the stars. I remember singing with him at the talent show. I treasure those moments. I do not want to let them go.

Memories, too, give us strength and wisdom. We can make a better decision when we think, "What would my loved one have wanted me to do?" We can be better parents when we remember our parents and what they taught us. Even their mistakes can help us if we remember and learn from them.

The author Anne Michaels once wrote that each act of memory is a "brick of potential thrown into the future." She means that when we remember, we create the potential for a future that can be better than the past. Memories are like seeds planted in the spring. They can bloom in the summer of our lives. That memories are both sweetness and pain is a mystery to me as deep as the abyss. It calls to mind the mystery of the liturgy, which states, "God kills and brings to life and too is the source of our salvation."

Earlier this morning, I sat at Kikar Zion and wondered what I would say this morning. We are supposed to see ourselves as if God personally redeemed each and every one of us from Egypt, but I have not felt that way this year. Struggling with my confusion in the wake of Joel's death, I was not sure how I would make sense for you of what I could not understand myself. I opened this book of responsa by Rabbi Ephraim Oshry—questions he was asked and answered during the *Shoah* sixty years ago.

As rabbi of the Kovno ghetto, Rabbi Oshry was asked unbelievable questions. "What blessing does one recite before going to one's death as a martyr? Were there circumstances in which suicide would not be regarded as a sin?" On Passover, he was asked, "Could tea be used instead of wine for the four cups drunk at the Passover Seder?" Could the black beans that were part of the ghetto food ration be eaten on Passover?" Filthy potato peels were to be mixed with a bit of flour to make *matza*. "Could the filthy peels be scrubbed with water—a leavening agent?" he was asked. The very asking and answering of these questions was an act of faith in the depths of hell.

Last year, Joel was here for only half the holiday because he needed to return home for more treatments to battle the cancer that would take his life. Knowing that he might die, that he might leave his wife and children behind, Joel led us in the Passover Seder. He fought with his final breath to stay alive and fulfill his dream of being a rabbi.

The memory of those who kept faith in the midst of hell is a gift, a challenge, to all of us. Their questions are our holy inheritance, a flashlight that shines through history into a dark room. They can help us find our way. Their enduring faith is a challenge to ours: we must never despair. This Passover, I may not feel I was taken out of Egypt, but I was. I need only remember the Jews of Kovno, and Joel, to know God's presence can be found even when darkness is all around. As we rise to say the memorial prayer, may their memories be a guiding light for us, and may they be for a blessing, always.

My answer? Joel's Passover and the holy Jews of Kovno. Each persevered through pain, kept faith amidst their suffering. They did not walk away, nor despair so much that they stopped observing Jewish law. Neither was their faith blind or easy. From within the tradition, they wrestled and questioned even, especially, as life tested them most. They returned to God, again and again. If their faith cracked, it was never broken.

3

Theology—Knowing God a Different Way

Maimonides once said that we can say nothing more about God other than what God is *not*. Better to be silent. Saying what God *is* places me apart from God, makes me an observer of Him, like a doctor who dissects a body; the doctor may know a lot about the cadaver, but only because he is dead. Knowledge at the cost of relationship. Is God all-good? Is God all-powerful? Is God all-knowing? Is the evil real? I do not want to know anymore. I reject the questions.

But there is another way of knowing; philosophers call it relational knowledge, like how we know another person, a friend. If I told you Jay was short, had blond hair and fair skin, or that Joel once had long hair and a beard, you might know more about them, but you wouldn't know them any better. There is a way we know that isn't about what can be measured or proven; it is the product of our experiences. I knew Jay and Joel because we spent time together; we talked and laughed, shared our joys and fears. We knew what made each other tick.

When I first encountered God in a ravine in the desert beneath the stars, it was not a philosophical discovery. It was an experience, the beginning of a relationship. The more that I prayed or kept Shabbat, studied Torah or simply walked through God's world; the more I sought meaning in my life, the better I knew God, and the more known I felt by Him. The Bible tells us that Adam "knew Eve." It means Adam had sex with Eve, but the sex was only a physical expression of a deeper emotional intimacy, a knowing that is the result of shared vulnerability, of risk, of openness and honesty. This knowing is the deep love of relationship over time. This is the kind of knowledge I desire of God. As my homiletics teacher taught me long ago, love is the result of holding one another, even God, not just when life is good. It is to love another even, perhaps especially, when we feel angry and confused and lost.

Do I know that God is all-good, all-powerful, all-knowing? I do not. I do not know what God is, but searching for answers as to what God is, trying to arrive at a thorough description of God's qualities and essences, is like that doctor performing an autopsy. I am sure Joel and the Jews of Kovno wondered about God, perhaps even were consumed by these questions. But they moved beyond them, did not let them be a stumbling block towards a relationship with their Creator. They moved beyond asking what God is.

I do not want to know about God anymore. I want to know God, for in trying to know Him, I believe there is a faith which can endure.

4

Joy and Tears

Why Ranon Jay? Why joy and Jay when so much of Jay's life was filled with so much pain? For one, because despite, or perhaps because, of everything Jay had to go through, he was a source of true joy. Especially in health, when Jay was playing piano or singing along to Billy Joel and Elton John, Jay was truly having a good time. Jay had had cancer in middle school. In high school, he gave all of us a healthy sense of perspective at a young age. When he was having a good time, it wasn't from an empty, "let's party" sort of place. Jay's joy came from deep places. It came from knowing life is fragile and fleeting. When he could sing, Jay sang a true song.

Jay's joy reminds me how the Jewish tradition's quintessential holiday of happiness and joy is Sukkot, when we sit outdoors in a sukkah, a flimsy hut. Psalm 145 begins, "Happy are those who dwell in Your house." On Sukkot, God's house is not a mighty Temple, but a fragile shelter with a view to the stars. A sukkah is a reminder that all other houses, no matter how big and sturdy, will one day fade away. Jay's joy is why, at a Jewish wedding, we break a glass, recalling sadness, not to dampen our joy but to deepen it, with perspective.

True happiness is not found at parties or on a quiet beach. Joy is not easy. It requires staring into the darkness to which attention must be paid.

Joy requires knowing the darkness—like one knows a friend or a lover, like Adam knew Eve. Through lenses filtered by pain, we learn to treasure great moments. We learn gratitude for the ordinary. This was Jay's gift to me. From his hospital bed he wrote,

> I still feel very lucky. Despite the despair of my situation, a side of me feels incredibly fortunate. After all, I have two homes and parents who love me and want me around. We can afford to have Fred [his nurse] and hospital beds and a van to get around. I don't worry about my next meal or getting shot walking down the street. Not everybody can say these things. Sure, I want to walk and want my independence and life back the way it was, but that is no longer the case. I'd like to know what the future holds, but I don't. Am I going to be like this forever? Could I get better? Will I live for six more months? I don't know.

Unable to walk, having touched "normal life" for just a few short months in college and at a job in London, and then having it ripped away from him, Jay still had perspective beyond his 24 years. He knew suffering and pain and, because he did, he knew joy, gratitude, even laughter. He continued,

> On a lighter note, most importantly, NORTHWESTERN BEAT MICHIGAN!!! At Ann Arbor. Wow! 4–1, undefeated in the Big 10. Can you name any team, ever, that beat Notre Dame and Michigan on the road in the same season? Neither can I. Well, I'm off and running (figuratively) to try and look like I do something. Fair thee well. Peace. Jay.

5

June, 2008. Camp Ramah, Ojai, CA

Staff Week. 250 counselors and program specialists—lifeguards, art and Hebrew teachers, basketball coaches—all gather at Ramah the week before camp begins. They bond with each other, learn the camp rules, review our mission, and plan for the kids' arrival. Shabbat during staff week is extra special. For the rest of the summer, the staff will be creating Shabbat for the kids at the same time as they try to have their own experience.

During staff week, the atmosphere at Friday evening prayers is pure *ruach* (Hebrew for "energy," "spirit," or "enthusiasm," and also "wind"). The staff can enjoy Shabbat all for themselves.

Everyone gathers in the chapel—the same room where I spoke at Yizkor on Passover a few months before. People sit on benches tightly packed together. They stand against the walls on the side and in the back. They overflow onto The Hill. I am standing in a sea of bodies in the middle of the room by the leader's table. I put on a tallit, face the ark and begin to lead Kabbalat Shabbat—a series of six psalms and the mystical prayer Lecha Dodi with which we will welcome the "Sabbath queen." The room swells with gentle harmonies and pulses with drums. We sing niggunim, wordless melodies that repeat, grow in intensity, and then softly fade until the next one begins. Kabbalat Shabbat concludes. In a few minutes, Ma'ariv, the evening prayer, will begin. A quiet settles over the room. I walk to the other side of the leader's table, face the community, and prepare to begin my D'var Torah.

I look down and Joel's memory returns to me again. Two summers ago, he was here to share this moment with me. Last summer, this very minute, I offered a prayer for his recovery. How is it possible he is gone?

When I finished speaking at Passover a few months before, I felt better, but I had gained enough wisdom to realize the grieving process was not over. To heal doesn't mean the pain goes away; just that one feels other things too. I could see the world in a more balanced way now; I had learned to focus on both death and life.

I stare at my notes, think of Joel, and feel tears well up again behind my eyes. I look up and scan the room filled with hundreds of young adults. I gaze at familiar faces. They look to me for inspiration. Their eyes share eagerness and anticipation; another summer will soon begin. I take a breath and begin to speak again.

> We all know the story of this week's parsha [the portion of the Torah read during the Shabbat day service]. The spies went to the land of Israel, brought back a bad report, and for that, they were punished. Is it fair? Rabbi Menachem Mendel of Kotzk wonders, "Why were they punished?" He argues, "Why should the spies be punished for telling the truth of what they experienced? The spies reported, 'We saw giants there, sons of huge ones, and we seemed like grasshoppers in our own eyes, and so we were in their eyes too' (Number 13:33). The giants were huge. The spies felt afraid. Should they have lied about their own experience?"

But the spies, explains the Kotzker, didn't just report their own experience; they purported to know what the giants thought of them too. Not lying is not the same as telling the truth. There is a truth beyond our own experience of things. The spies did not lie, but to tell the truth about something important, to see beyond your own perception of things, you must go deeper within yourself; you must explore your own assumptions. The sin of the spies is that they did not dig deeper; they did not understand that their fear about their own weakness biased their report about the land. To tell the truth, we must dig deeper. We can't give up.

Depth is hard. It is harder to think than to watch television. It is harder to read a book than to watch a movie. It is harder to have faith when things don't make sense. It is harder to be married than to date around, but that's what love is.

There is a story about a rich man who has a beautiful daughter. He travels to the yeshiva to find her a husband and tells the head of the yeshiva that the student who can answer his question will marry his daughter. Each of the students try to answer the rich man's question but each one fails and is sent away. The rich man gets into his carriage and begins to drive away when one student waves his hands, runs and screams for him to stop. The rich man leans out the window of his carriage and asks, "Do you know the answer?"

"No," the young man says. "But I cannot let you leave without knowing the answer."

"You are the one," says the rich man, "who will marry my daughter." The student understands that one must never give up, never despair.

Chevre [friends], it has been a long and difficult year. I am thinking, of course, of our dear friend Joel for whose recovery we prayed one year ago tonight, but who died in November. Arriving to this moment was not easy for me. The journey taught me we must never despair. We must always dig deeper. We must always continue to pray, to search, to strive for a relationship with God.

As you work with the kids this summer, there will be moments that try your patience; times when you'll wonder if you're doing any good. Remember to go deeper. Be persistent. The kids need to know you will never give up on them. By sticking with them, you will find a great treasure—a holy soul just waiting to be discovered. Dig deep—that is where the truth is found.

6

July-August, 2008, Camp Ramah in California

The summer continues. Joel's memory doesn't disappear from my mind—I wouldn't want it to—but I can move forward more truthfully. During the year, when I interviewed the girl in my office for a counselor position, questions about God and suffering burned inside me. But if I had blurted them out, they would have made no sense to her, or others, who were not in such pain. When I went to camp for a winter weekend and took some prospective camp parents on a tour of the tree house, I wanted to tell them how it was the place I visited with my friend Joel who was dead. But I hardly think they would have enrolled their children for the summer! During the year, I was, in a sense, living a lie, putting on a face for the world so I could live in it. In some ways that is what grief requires, to push oneself back into the world; even, perhaps especially, when one would rather be alone. Over the summer, I am able to return to myself and to being the rabbi I want to be.

As rabbi of the camp, I don't just run services and give sermons. I visit tents and bunks, tell bedtime stories and sing lullabies. I teach the staff in small groups and lead *birkat hamazon*—the grace after meals—in the *chadar ochel*, the dining room. One night, I hike in the dark to visit the youngest campers on their campout at the tree house. We deliver snacks for the staff, look in on the sleeping children and chat for a while underneath a blanket of stars. One of the counselors plays guitar. I think of Joel, but I smile and enjoy myself too. Some other counselors and I sing along.

The end of the summer approaches. On the last night of camp, everyone dresses in costume and gathers in the chadar ochel for a festive "banquet." As a special treat, caffeine-free Coca-Cola is served with dinner. We sing birkat hamazon and the music staff leads the camp in singing our entire repertoire of fun Jewish songs, followed by a song for each age group, then our camp song, and finally Himnon Ramah—the hymn of Ramah camps all over the country. Kids bang on the tables, dance around the chadar ochel. The singing goes on for over an hour. When it's over, we get the kids settled down and crowd into one half of the dining room for the end of session video to celebrate the summer. The lights are dimmed.

Hundreds of campers and counselors grow quiet as the following words scroll slowly from the top to the bottom of the screen:

> As our Rosh Musica during the 2005 and 2006 summers, Joel Shickman shared his love of music with the campers and staff of Camp Ramah in California. Through his music and presence, he brought joy and light to Ramah. Last summer, we prayed for his recovery but on November 17, 2007, Joel left this world and took his place amongst the choir of God's angels. Our teacher, Reb Mimi Feigelson, teaches, "some people are very present in their absence," and so has it been for us this summer at camp. In every song under the big oak tree, in the chadar ochel and at the amphitheater, we have missed you, Joel, and we will carry you in our hearts always.
>
> In Joel's memory, may we continue to sing. May his memory be for a blessing, always.

The words stop for a moment, fade away, and, for a moment, everyone sits silently in the dark. I inhale deeply and slowly breathe out. Someone touches me gently on the shoulder from behind, the video begins, and the children begin to shout and cheer.

7

Last Day of Camp, 2008

Banquet ends and the youngest campers stay up later than normal. They eat candy late at night, run around camp in the dark with their counselors and enjoy their last night as a time and place they can do lots of things their parents won't let them do at home during the year. For the older campers, the last night of camp is much more bittersweet. It is fun. But they realize much more: the summer is over. School will soon begin. Tomorrow they will say good-bye.

The oldest campers bring sleeping bags and "camp out" by age group, 9th graders on the floor of the Whizin building, 10th graders on the floor of the chapel. They will talk late into the night, holding on to the precious moments of their summer just a little longer before they finally fall asleep. For the campers in the Machon Edah—the group of campers entering 10th grade—it is an especially hard night; they are not just leaving one another. As campers, they are leaving Ramah for the last time. A part of their childhood is ending.

Around midnight I enter the chapel, wade through pillows and sleeping bags, and sit down against the wall amongst the counselors. The lights are off. In the middle of the room, dozens of tea light candles flicker. A camper takes her turn speaking to the group.

> I will never forget you all. I can't believe it's over. Machon '08 was the best edah in the history of Camp Ramah and this has been the best summer of my life. We may not all be totally best friends, but I know every person here cares about each other and we will be there for each other forever. I will love you forever.

She finishes speaking and the group softly snaps their fingers, signaling agreement and love. In a moment, another person starts to speak. It goes on like this for hours. Year after year, I hear kids talk like this. It never fails to move me: the intensity of the feelings, the sadness as a journey comes to an end. Even with the best of intentions, their friendships will never be the same. The end is more permanent than they know. Around 2:00 AM, I head home to get some sleep. I will talk to Machon in the morning.

Around 6:00 AM, I get dressed and prepare a pot of coffee. I pour one cup for myself and a second for the unit head of Machon, who is exhausted from being up most of the night. I take my tallit and tefillin and head to the chapel where Machon will pray Shacharit together for the last time. My custom is to lead the prayers and then speak to the campers before they go to breakfast and board the buses to go home, their last moments alone as a group at camp. There is a story I always tell.

> Abraham waits at the edge of his tent to welcome guests. Three angels tell him that Sarah will soon be blessed in her old age with a child. Always trying to make guests feel welcome, Abraham tells Sarah to prepare some cakes for lunch and runs off to the herd to find a calf to serve their honored guests. The Torah says Abraham returns and Sarah, Abraham and the three angels eat lunch. But in the Zohar, the foundational work of Jewish mysticism, something happens to Abraham before he returns to eat. He goes on a journey.
>
> When Abraham runs to the herd to get a calf, the calf runs away. Abraham chases the calf into a cave, but it is not just any cave. It is the Cave of Machpelah—the cave where Abraham, Issac and Jacob, Sarah, Rebecca and Leah will be buried. In the cave, accord-

ing the Zohar, Abraham finds a river, but not just any river. It is a river of light. It leads to the Garden of Eden, to paradise, back to God. Abraham achieves what no person ever could: he returns to Eden.

The Bible tells us God placed angels and "a flaming, revolving sword to guard the path leading to the Tree of Eternal Life" (Genesis 3:24), but Abraham somehow makes it past. Abraham arrives. One can see him sitting there basking in God's love, enjoying a sense of fulfillment and rest after all life's troubles.

What I don't say to the kids this morning—it is hard enough already for them to leave camp—is how Abraham's journey to his burial place reminds me of the journey to the funeral. The river of light doesn't only illuminate; it can blind too. When Joel died, I was unable to stop thinking about his death, to see beyond the terrifying truth of the grave. Like a whirlpool, there is something tempting about grief, as if one fulfills a noble duty by living in memory and ignoring the world. But I need to let him go. I need to return to the living world.

The story could end there. But one my teachers, Rabbi Lawrence Kushner, points out that in the Torah, the story continues. How does Abraham return? Rabbi Kushner imagines Abraham sitting in the Garden of Eden, enjoying himself for a moment when, suddenly, he hears someone calling, "Abe? Abraham? Where are you?" It is Sarah. "The guests are waiting. Are you coming?" At that moment, Rabbi Kushner says, Abraham is faced with a challenge: Should he remain in the Garden, at one with God, but alone? Or should he return to the world he left so he can eat lunch with his wife and their guests? But, Rabbi Kushner explains, here's the trick: if Abraham chooses to remain in paradise, he will lose paradise. But if he chooses to leave, Abraham will have it forever.

What does it mean? Why do I tell you that story on your last morning as campers at Ramah? First, because while Camp Ramah is not perfect, I do hope it has been a sort of paradise for you. I hope in your journey as a camper at Ramah you have felt God's presence for the first time. I hope you have experienced a vision of what is possible and good in the world. I hope Ramah has been a place you could be the sort of Jew and the sort of human being you want to be. But now, only at the very end, can I tell you the secret:

And, without fail, every session, every summer, I look into the campers' eyes and tears well up in mine as I say the following words:

The whole reason you come to camp . . . is to leave.

Some campers, even some counselors who have heard this lesson many times before, softly begin to cry. Gently, I continue.

> We love you. We love taking care of you and see in you possibility and hope for everything that can be made good in the world. But. If you were to stay here at camp, something great will have been lost. A great potential unfilled. But if you leave, then not only will you have this summer forever, you will bring goodness into a broken world sorely in need. Tzeitchem L'Shalom—go in peace dear ones, and may God bless you along the way.

I wipe the tears from my eyes. Some announcements are made and the final prayer is sung. I hug some of the kids at the door and we make our way down to breakfast. The buses are waiting. In a few hours, everyone is gone and Jen and the boys and I are alone at camp.

8

After Camp, 2008

When I was young and swam all the time, I didn't need to think about my body. It was healthy. I was strong and thought it would last forever. Death reminds us that it won't; that we will all return to dust. But grief, like youth, contains its own misperception about the body: that death and decay is all there is. I am trying to find a balance now. There is death and decay. I see that. But there is life too. My body is growing older, but it can heal. There are tears, and there is joy.

A life coach once told me, "you need to exercise," but not for the reason I expected. I thought she was going to tell me I needed to lose weight. "You need activities in your life that center you," she said, "and to do that, you need to focus on your breathing, on your breath." Interesting. When I swim by myself, I warm up and often continue with a set where I will breathe every three strokes for eight lengths, then every five strokes for eight lengths, then every seven strokes for eight lengths, or some iteration of breath control over a distance. Sometimes it gives me a headache, but often, when I don't think about other things and just concentrate on my breathing, I feel better when I'm done.

The summer is over. I have been out of balance, stretched like a chord, pulled thin, like pizza dough poorly kneaded, extended in too many directions by too many people. My sons are full of feelings—happy to have me to themselves again, angry that I was present in camp yet absent and unavailable to them for so long. Jen alternates between wanting to help me recover from my physical and emotional exhaustion, to give me a break and some solitude after a summer she sees taking its toll and, on the other hand, handing me the children and taking a break herself, needing me as a husband and a father again.

We head out with our bikes on the long path downhill from Ojai to the ocean. This bike ride is a healthy compromise. I have taken the boys from their ima for an hour out of camp, giving her the break she desires and deserves. The boys' little wheels spin fast, and I guide them through the stop signs and oncoming bikers. Halfway to the ocean, we meet their mother at a Shell station. The boys get sodas for their car ride uphill back to camp, and Jen takes them away so that I can have some time to be alone, to exercise, to concentrate on my breath.

I shift into a lower gear and begin to pump at a steady speed. A view of the mountains and valley opens up to my left. The weakening evening sun eases lower towards the horizon. My body warms up and begins to sweat. I turn off the bike path and wind on a quiet country road. It climbs gently alongside a riverbed reserve, dotted with small, unassuming houses unchanged by a world of strip malls and prefab housing developments.

My pedaling is regular, and I focus on my breathing. I exhale carbon dioxide every three pedal rotations and make room for the oxygen my muscles need. Exhale, pedal, pedal, pedal, exhale, pedal, pedal, pedal. I feel my chest. Joel's memory returns, the rhythm of his breath kept steady by a ventilator many months ago.

"Joel," I say between breaths into the quiet afternoon. I am uninterested in the theological, philosophical and academic problems raised by the fact that I am speaking to him. "I miss you, Joel." Exhale, pedal, pedal, pedal. Where is Joel, I wonder, now that he is dead?

It is not so commonly known that, while Jewish life focuses on this world, not the next, Jewish tradition does in fact affirm an afterlife. The rabbis called it, "The World to Come." Some texts pronounce a belief in resurrection; the belief that, in some future age, the dead will rise from their graves and live again. Other texts speak of the reincarnation of the soul in new bodies. Other rabbis imagine that, in the World to Come, "there is no eating nor drinking nor sexual intercourse nor business nor jealousy nor hatred nor competition, but the righteous sit with their crowns on their heads feasting on the splendor of God's presence" (Bera-khot 17a).

The Hasidim teach that death is like a drop of water returning to the ocean. The water is a drop, separate from the ocean, just as we are separate from God while we are alive. When we die, we do not cease to be, just like the water of the drop doesn't cease to be when it returns to the water; the drop still exists, only it isn't separate anymore. I imagine Joel has returned to the Oneness of the world; that he is nowhere but everywhere.

On my right, I pass a large property where they board horses. The air is filled with the scent of livestock and manure. "Maybe people who have died are in the smells of the world," I imagine. I laugh out loud: I can think of some people who are in the manure. Joel is not in the manure! But where is he?

Sometimes the word "where" can mean not the directional where, but where as in "why is someone absent?" God's first question to Adam after he ate from the tree is, "Where are You?" God knows where Adam is. He is asking, "Why are you not here? Why are you hiding? Why are you suddenly scared to be in my presence?" God does not want Adam to hide. His question is an invitation. When Cain kills Abel, God asks, "Where is Abel, your brother?" Again, God knows where Abel is. His question is both an invitation to confess and an accusation. God asks "Why is Abel absent? Why is he not here? Why is he dead?"

I have struggled for many months to try and understand, "Why is Joel dead? Why isn't he here? Why isn't he riding a bike with me after the summer?" Curiously, at this moment, that is not my question. Instead, I wonder where, directionally, Joel is. In what location might I find him now that he is dead? Is he in the smell of the orange trees that dot the Ojai valley? Is he in the salty breeze off the ocean waters? Is he in my breath as I pump the pedals and ride uphill while the sun goes down? Can he move, skipping from person to person, wiping tears away?

Today I imagine he is in the smell of the huge oak tree at camp in whose shade he would play music and teach children to sing with joy and love. I imagine that during the summer, he perched himself amidst its branches and leaves. I imagine him in the breath of sweet harmonies sung by children. Today, the children have gone home. Perhaps Joel remains amidst the tree in the stillness of camp. Or maybe, as the summer ended, he allowed himself to be swept away by the wind, so he could look in on Heather and the boys.

"I miss you Joel," I say again to the air. I imagine maybe I am breathing him into myself, pedal, pedal, pedal. I want to inhale deeply and carry him in my lungs and muscles, in my brain and blood, in my heart and hands. I want to carry him with me and not lose him again as the real, flesh and blood, Joel fades and is replaced by memory.

"Where are you, Joel?" I ask again to the air. Tears stream down my face, mixing with sweat. Is he here? I stop, lean against my bike along the side of the road, and squint into the sun as it sets beyond the valley below.

Epilogue

"Those who sow in tears, they will reap in joy." (Psalm 130)

SINCE THE TIME OF the Torah, Jews have marked a grave with a stone or monument. After Rachel died, we learn, "Jacob erected a monument on Rachel's grave" (Genesis 35:20). One common practice is that the tombstone is put in place and an unveiling ceremony is held one year after a loved one dies. The ceremony involves the recitation of a few psalms, the unveiling of the headstone, the *El Maleh Rachamim* memorial prayer, the *kaddish*, and the sharing of memories about the one who died. Sunday, November 16, 2008 is the unveiling for Joel; one year minus one day since he died.

Jennifer and I spend Shabbat in Los Angeles. When Shabbat ends an hour after sundown, we travel to the airport, and catch another late night flight to Dallas. We even stay at the same hotel where, one year before, I stayed up late feeling grateful not to be the rabbi performing Joel's funeral, doubtful if I was fit to be a rabbi any more, and wondering if I could ever find words to comfort others when it was I who was in so much pain. Tomorrow, I will speak as Joel's friend, and as a rabbi too. I have room for both of these parts of myself. As we get settled into our room, the sadness returns, but I am able to sleep.

The drive out to the old cemetery feels familiar. We wind our way across town, past old drugstores and poor churches, and enter through the iron cemetery gate. We're early. Heather and the boys are the only other ones there and I'm grateful to spend some quiet time with them before others arrive. Her boys wander curiously amongst the headstones. Heather and I hug. A year after Jay died, I never returned to his grave, never saw his headstone nor the grass that grew where he lay. Standing at Joel's grave, I am comforted by the memory that at his funeral a year ago, we buried him right; we sweat through our shirts and tucked him in to sleep, did what friends do for a brother. I am here with Heather, where I should be, keeping a promise made to Joel in his final moments. I look down—grass has grown where the dirt was before.

I remember our hugs at Cedars Sinai and City of Hope. It hurt so much. It has been such an excruciating year, but I feel a scar beginning to form. The cemetery's old graves bear witness not only to the searing pain of a funeral, but to the gentle sadness and resignation that come years later. The journey will continue. Life will never be the same, but joy and laughter are possible too.

Coleman wanders amongst the headstones

During the past year, I read a few books about the journey through grief. One entitled, "Against the Dying of the Light," was written by Leonard Fein, a well-known author and teacher who founded *Moment Magazine* in the 1970s. Fein wrote his book after the death of his daughter, Nomi. Towards the end of the book, he writes a letter to his granddaughter, Liat, who will grow up without a mother.

> I want for you, my love, flesh of my flesh and bone of my bone, that you will be whole. The emptiness cannot be wished away, nor is there reason to try. All we need guard against is the swelling of the emptiness, its displacement of the other truths of our lives. You are the daughter of a mother who died just 500 days after you were born. But for sure her story did not end in January of 1996. Her death is a sorry fact of your life—but not, I pray, the defining fact. There is much, much more to her story than the tragedy of her death—and all that is yours, too."

Heather will always be a woman whose loving husband died too soon. Coleman and Miles and Ellis will always be sons of a wonderful father they did not know enough. Joel and I could have raised our children together. Those are things that will never go away, but the story also goes on. "Joy comes in the morning," says the psalmist. I squeeze Heather, close my eyes and hope she will always remember the other truths of our lives: "The emptiness cannot be wished away…all we need guard against is the swelling of the emptiness."

When everyone arrives, we awkwardly call across the gravestones and invite them over to Joel's grave. Shearith Israel's Rabbi Gershon is here; he speaks about Joel, recites Psalm 23 and asks Heather to unveil the headstone. It reads, "Beloved husband, father, teacher and friend. Joel Nathan Shickman. December 25, 1969. November 17, 2007." There is a guitar, musical notes, and the Hebrew letters "tav, nun, tzadi, beit, and heh" which stands for "Tehei Nishmato Tzrur B'tzrur Hahaim"—"may his soul be bound up in the bonds of life." At the bottom it reads, "Sing unto God a new song." While the cantor chants the memorial prayer, *El Maleh Rahamim*, the wind blows through the leaves. I think about Joel amidst the giant oak tree at camp.

The *kaddish* prayer does not mention death; it is a prayer that praises God's great and holy name. Jewish tradition requires the Mourner's Kaddish to be said for eleven months, not twelve. Eleven months because some sources believe that the saying of the *kaddish* helps the soul of the one who has died to rise and make its way to heaven, a process that, for a lesser person, should take a full year. To say *kaddish*, then, for all twelve months would be to say that our loved one was somehow less worthy. So we stop at eleven months, confident that their deeds in this world surely were sufficient to raise them to heaven. Heather stopped saying *kaddish* a month ago; in a moment, Rabbi Gershon will turn to Heather and invite her to say it for the first time in a month. It will be her last *kaddish* in the year mourning Joel's death.

The *kaddish* begins, "May God's great name expand and be sanctified," and the community responds, "Amen." It continues with a prayer that this happen soon and, then, in the second half of the prayer, there is a list of eight adjectives describing how praiseworthy is God's name: "Blessed, and praised, glorified, exalted, extolled, mighty, upraised, and lauded be the Name of the Holy Blessing One." Then, after all those adjectives, we say God's name is "*L'eyla min kol birchata v'shirata…*"—it is "beyond any blessing or song, praise and consolation that can be uttered in this world." One could ask, "If God's name is beyond anything that can be said, why even try? Why say the *kaddish* at all? Wouldn't it be better to remain silent and say nothing?"

On one level, it's true. Sometimes we talk too much and forget the power of silence. But there is also power in trying, because in our aspiration to say something true, in refusing to be silenced, in continuing to try to break through our limitations, holiness occurs. . .even as you know in your effort, "God is beyond this too."

One final question: "Why do we ask mourners to say a special *kaddish*?" One of my teachers, Rabbi Mordecai Finley, once told a story about how he thinks the practice came to be. One day someone stood up to lead the prayers. When the leader arrived to the *kaddish*, a mourner walked into the back of the room. The person leading the service thought about the words "May God's great name expand and be sanctified." Then he thought about the mourner who just walked in, and how difficult it would be for the mourner to hear those words. More than anyone in the room, that mourner would be tempted to say, "There is no holiness; there is no righteousness; there is no truth."

In that moment, imagines Rabbi Finley, the community turned to the mourner and said, "we can't say this without you. You are the one who must lead us, for if you can say, 'May God's great name expand and be sanctified,' if you can fight through the darkness and silence and pain, if you can summon the courage and declare even now that holiness is pushing itself into the world, that the holiness is beyond anything that can be named or expressed, then you can get us there." To heal from grief does not mean we no longer feel the loss. To heal is to ache for our loved one and to find the courage to see and declare, "Grief is not all there is." It is to fight through darkness and declare, "God's holiness is pushing its way into the world."

"*Yitgadal v'yitkadash Shmei Rabbah*"—"May God's great name expand and be sanctified," Heather says. We all answer, "Amen."

When she finishes, Rabbi Gershon asks me to me to speak. I remember my silence at Jay's funeral so long ago, my confusion and pain dormant for so many years. I think about Joel and the year which has passed. I think about the prayers and the holidays, the study and the struggle to return here to his grave, to be able to speak again. I see now my brokenness and confusion are not things I need to hide or deny. They are strengths, not weaknesses. Having known darkness, I am stronger. I can speak in a way I couldn't before. I take a piece of paper out of my suit jacket pocket and begin.

> *Saving Private Ryan* is an Academy Award-winning film that chronicles the brutal battles of early World War II. It tells the story of a heroic search by a band of American soldiers to bring home a last living son, Private James Ryan, to his mother who has already lost three of her four sons. The movie's battle scenes conclude with a dramatic last stand to defend a vital bridge, and then the film flashes forward.
>
> Years later, Private Ryan walks amidst thousands of graves at the Normandy American Cemetery & Memorial, where his comrades-in-arms are buried. His family walks behind him as he wanders alone in contemplation and sorrow. Now old and fragile, Ryan collapses at the grave of his commander 50 years hence. His family runs towards him, helps him to his feet. His younger children look stunned and helpless as their brave father cries openly. Ryan turns to his wife and says, "Tell me I've led a good life."

I pause for a moment, breathe in and then exhale deeply and slowly. Jen squeezes my left hand. The paper quivers in my right hand as I look down at Joel's grave. This, I think to myself, is the question I returned to ask Joel: tell me, my friend who can no longer live, who would have helped me to live my life better had we raised our children together; tell me if I have lived my life well, if I have made you proud. I look up and continue.

> "What?" Ryan's wife asks him.
>
> "Tell me I'm a good man," he asks again.
>
> "Of course you are," she comforts him, clearly puzzled. How could he think otherwise? Where did such a question come from?
>
> Here we stand again in this old Jewish cemetery outside of Dallas. Private Ryan's question at the cemetery in Normandy is one I understand more deeply in the year since Joel died. It is the question carried by those who remain alive when a friend dies, a burden borne by the living, simply because they live. The question echoes from beyond the curtain that separates this world and the next, from a silent unknown. It nudges me urgently from within, refusing to subside: "Have I lived a good life? Have I been a good husband? A good father? Have you done good, Daniel? Or have you wasted away precious time?" I hear these questions unendingly. In memories I cannot, nor would I want to, escape, Joel's

memory gently whispers to me: "You remain in the world. You've got to live for me, my friend."

A cloud gently passes overhead. Heather stands bravely with her boys. Our eyes meet. I breathe deeply once more, look down at the paper and continue.

> What comfort have we? Only to carry him with us, to be, as a Hasidic *rebbe* once taught, his hands in the world. As we do a *mitzvah* here on earth, we must reach to heaven, take Joel's dear hands that reach down and yearn to be with us, and be his partner, his hands in this world he can touch no longer. We must remember him and, through that memory, burst through the divide that stands immovably between us; we must refuse to let it be real, to let it divide us from him. We must remember him and live well.
>
> In the movie, Tom Hanks plays Captain John Miller, commander of the unit that has sacrificed so much so that Private Ryan will live. Miller lies dying on the bridge. He pulls Ryan to him and, with his final breath, tells him, "Earn this."
>
> Joel, I will try, my friend. Forgive me when I do not. Bless me when I do. And put in a good word for me. I miss you only a little less than I can bear.

Appendix—A Reluctant Guide

I RESISTED WRITING "TIPS" on how to grieve, as if there is a recipe one can follow for healing. There is not. If someone tries to tell you there is, check your pockets. Elizabeth Kubler-Ross wrote about how her stages of grief were misunderstood: "They were never meant to tuck messy emotions into neat packages. They are responses to loss that many people have, but there is not a typical response to loss, as there is no typical loss." I wrote a memoir of my journey, rather than a "guide to grieving," to respect the uniqueness of each loss, the singularity of every person's mourning. C.S. Lewis once wrote, "Grief needs a history, not a map." I tried to write a history hoping that by sharing my story, you might feel less alone. There is strength in companionship that can help light a way through darkness back to wholeness and life, but even when walking with a companion, each person must lift his/her own foot and put it down in front of the other.

I am a rabbi, from the Hebrew word which means "teacher," but I cannot give you answers. I caution you against those who promise God's truth, as if it is a product to be bought, sold, or given away. Teaching is rarely about a teacher deciding to *give* something to a student; rather it is about sharing of one's true self—one's hopes and fears, questions and answers, faith and doubt. In sharing a story, the teacher can help a student to understand his/her own story, but no one can do the work for you.

Yet in looking back, I can see some insights that guided me. Looking forward, I see now there are truths I believe in more deeply because they've been tested in the crucible of experience. The insights which follow may not work for you today, or tomorrow, or ever. But if they help you or anyone else to heal someday, then putting them to paper will have been worthwhile.

There is Nothing God Cannot Contain

The rabbis said: "God wants the heart." We can feel frustrated and angry at God; we can despair at life and cry out. God can contain those feelings. Often, people cannot. Do not be shushed by others' fear. People get nervous, like Job's comforters, when feelings are too raw, when questions get too pointed. John Milton wrote, "A man may be a heretic in the truth; if he believes things only because his Pastor says so, or the Assembly so determines, without knowing other reasons, though his belief be true, yet the very truth he holds becomes his heresy." Do not fear what others declare to be heresy; seek truth. The Talmud teaches that God's seal is truth. There is nothing God cannot contain that is true.

Find a Practice

As I wrote, one of the most painful parts of grieving for a friend is not being obligated to say *kaddish*. Our grief is real. If our traditions do not obligate us, we should obligate ourselves. If you worry, as I did, what other people will think if you say *kaddish* when you are not the relative of someone who died, don't. If someone asks, "Why are you saying *kaddish*?" answer them, "I lost a friend and am saying *kaddish* to honor them and help me grieve." Taking on an obligation to a practice is a critical part of healing. Whether by saying *kaddish*, going to church, seeing a therapist, writing in a journal, participating in a grief group, or another choice, obligate yourself to a regular practice.

Why is it so important? Such practices create space for us to mourn; they prevent us from cruising back into life and deceiving ourselves into believing that our grief is done before it is. Human beings are masters at self-deception. Grief is hard. Of all the things we go through in life—divorce, loss of a job, painful dissolution of a friendship—only bereavement due to death is accounted for in the standard clinical assessment for situational grief. Doctors say situational grief lasts for six months to three years. Trying to avoid grief or "power through it" without acknowledging its deep effect on your life is like digging a channel in the sand at the seashore; eventually the water is going get through. Our sadness will manifest itself in unhealthy ways, in anger at our loved ones, in overindulgence. After Aaron's sons die, God tells him that priests must not drink wine or other intoxicants when they fulfill their priestly duties (Leviticus

10:8). According to rabbinic tradition, the juxtaposition is purposeful: God warns Aaron against masking his sorrow with alcohol.

A regular practice does not mean a consistent experience. You need not cry each time you're in the therapist's office. You shouldn't expect to have a religious epiphany every time you pray. Rather, a regular practice provides a mirror to understanding your journey. By walking the same path through the woods, you will not only notice small changes in the trees, but small changes in yourself. A practice can signal, "this week, I'm doing fine," as much as it can be an outlet for days when you're not. What it does most is prevent us from trying to avoid something that should not be avoided.

A structured practice can also propel you forward. Having a practice that you do precisely when you don't feel the need for it, or want to do it, provides a means to push you beyond your comfort zone; it forces you to give up trying to control a process that cannot be controlled, only understood.

Seek Community

It is true: each person's grief is unique, and nobody can quite understand what you're going through. But that's not the only truth. Your grief may be unique, but you also need not be alone. Jewish tradition requires *kaddish* to be said with a minimum of ten adult Jews, in part to draw the mourner away from the temptation to escape. You may want to be alone—that's okay sometimes, even for a while. One can be alone without being lonely. But being alone while you grieve, isolating yourself from those who love you, may be a red flag that something deeper is wrong. Seek help—from friends, from community, from a therapist. Part of returning to a healthy life is returning to a world of relationships.

Jewish tradition prohibits mourners from attending festive parties and live music concerts. One reason may be because of the dissonance between the sadness we feel and the powerful joy at these events. But another reason may be because at concerts and parties, we become "lost in the crowd," anonymous in a sea of people. Attending church or synagogue, inviting close friends to dinner, or accepting an offer to go for a hike or participate in a class, however, is different. When we are surrounded by friends and doing activities that enable true fellowship, we are beckoned to return from the cocoon of our grief to the companionship of our fellow human beings.

Don't Rush Back In

One of the wisest rituals of the Jewish tradition is *shiva*, the requirement to put life on hold for seven days after a funeral and do nothing but grieve. Grief is going to happen. It's either going to fester beneath the surface because you denied it and went back to work, or you can grieve now. Don't try to rush to what can't be rushed. Be patient. Don't try to wish your way to being "done." Our histories do not disappear; our past is not wiped away. We carry our experiences with us, but grief need not define us. Context, time, and continuing to live life –these all heal, but they all take time.

Not Getting Lost in Grief

Don't rush, but don't get stuck either. You can grieve too much, too long, too deeply. Some instincts should be curbed, not because to feel them is wrong, but because it is short-sighted to make lasting decisions based upon them. Tattoos and cutting were forbidden by the Torah seemingly because they were inappropriate responses to grief and death: "You shall not make gashes in your flesh for the dead, or incise any marks on your-selves: I am Adonai" (Leviticus 19:28). Why? One reason may be because trying to externalize one's pain short circuits an internal process, the "soul work" of dealing with one's suffering. But tattoos and gashes also may be forbidden because they are (virtually) permanent. Why shouldn't we create a monument to our loved one on our skin? Because part of our job is not only to remember, but also to forget, to heal, to move on. Jewish tradition requires *shiva* for seven days, *shloshim* for thirty, *kaddish* for eleven months, the unveiling of a headstone at a year, and then, at major holidays in spring, summer and fall, a memorial service. Such a structure acknowledges the intensity of loss and gives our loved ones their rightful place in our lives. But it also defines when we must let go and move past the initial intensity of loss so that their memory does not deny our experi-ence of the present nor define our future.

Grief can also be selfish. Towards the end of his book, *Kaddish*, Leon Wieseltier writes how "human love must rise above animal love." He says, "[t]he difference [between the two] is in detachment." What I think he means by "animal love" is that instinctual, biological love between parents and children, between mother bears and their cubs. Even, and perhaps especially, in grief, we must remember to fight off the urge to love our loved one too much and, by doing so, to refuse to heal and forgive and move on. "In the heart of the family," writes Wieseltier, "there must be a wise alienation. . .a father, a mother, a son, a daughter: they, too, can be idols. Idolatry may be nothing more than too much love." One can grieve too much, make one's loss too much the center of one's life. Time and forgetting may seem cruel. We may feel the temptation never to marry again, to close ourselves up and never allow ourselves the vulnerability of love and relationship. Such a temptation should be fought. Dying with the one who died is no tribute to the one we loved in life.

A Final Thought—Grieving and Living

Faith Unravels was born out of the specific experience of mourning friends who died; in truth, we mourn all the time. We mourn paths not taken, people not known, choices we feared to make, parts of ourselves we did not have the courage to express. Learning to grieve is learning how to live with courage and dignity in the face of an existential truth: we die each moment. Things fade each moment in front of us, yet God bids us, "Choose life, so that you and your children may live" (Deuteronomy 30:19). That is our task.